THEY CALL ME PATHFINDER

For Josh,

THEY CALL ME PATHFINDER

Education—Basketball—Equality

Much Success!

By

MARK A EPSTEIN

Mark "Pathfinder" Epstein

ISBN: 9798662963436 (paperback)

DEDICATION

In Loving Memory of Robert S. Epstein

11-3-49 to 8-13-20

This book is written in memory of my precious brother Robert "Bobby-EPPY" Epstein. Bobby was my constant shining light. Bobby or EPPY as he was called fought valiantly to overcome a rare form of cancer over the course of this project. Bobby passed away a short time after this book was completed. I hope you enjoy the stories that are in this book that we shared.

Proceeds from this book and all donations will be donated under the name Robert "Bobby" Epstein to the Gene Upshaw Cancer Center where cancer research and treatment are ongoing.

To EPPY, with all my grateful love, forever your "Pathfinder."

TABLE OF CONTENTS

Testimonials		ix
Introduction		xi
Foreword		xiii
One	Black Like Me	1
Two	Pathfinder	11
Three	Time To Move On	33
Four	Goodbye	39
Five	In Search Of Myself In Charleston	43
Six	First Job	49
Seven	Blacks In Education	51
Eight	Where Is The Berry? 1989–1990	55
Nine	North Charleston High School, 1990–1993	77
Ten	The Citadel Graduate College, 1989–1993	85
Eleven	Friendships	89
Twelve	Playing The Single Life In Charleston	93
Thirteen	The Day My Life Restarted	99
Fourteen	James Island High Trojans, 1993–2001	103
Fifteen	West Ashley High Wildcats, 2001–2011	109
Sixteen	St. John's High, 2011–2014	117
Seventeen	A Wildcat Again, The Last Hurrah 2014-2015	125
Eighteen	Africa	133
Nineteen	Charlie Epstein Day	137
Twenty	Aren't You Bill Russell?	143

Twenty-One   "We've Come A Long Way, But We Still Have
              A Long Way To Go"   157
Twenty-Two   Closing Thoughts   163

Acknowledgments   165
Reviews and Endorsements   169

TESTIMONIALS

Coach Jim Calhoun is one of America's greatest college coaches of all time, having coached the University of Connecticut's Huskies to three men's NCAA basketball championships. Coach Calhoun writes, "Mark Epstein's story and book, *They Call Me Pathfinder: Education—Basketball—Equality*, are what our nation and country have been built on. For a lot of people in this country who enjoy sports and pray for equality, it is a great story, and Pathfinder's values and culture are what we all love about our game. This is a must read. You will enjoy the story and be inspired by the life lessons. Well done, Mark!"

Tom McMillen, all-American, Olympian, Rhodes scholar, longtime NBA star, congressman from Maryland, chairman of the President's Council on Sports and Fitness, says, "Mark Epstein, alias Pathfinder, takes the readers through an inspirational journey depicting how he persevered through many personal and educational setbacks in his hometown of Worcester, Massachusetts, by the values learned through basketball. Pathfinder shows tremendous courage later in life when he becomes a leader for equality for students in the Deep South. An incredible story that will inspire everyone to stand up for justice and equality."

Richard Lapchick, the world's top leader for diversity and ethics in global sport, also often known as the "Racial Conscience of Sport," writes, "*They Call Me Pathfinder: Education—Basketball—Equality* will inspire readers to stand up and work toward a nation where equality is real. Pathfinder shows tremendous determination as both an educator and civil rights activist to improve education for all in South Carolina. Read this book!"

Seth Greenberg, former college basketball coach and current host and lead commentator for ESPN college basketball, writes, "*They Call Me Pathfinder: Education—Basketball—Equality* is a story of one man's mission to impact the education system in South Carolina. The book encourages and exemplifies the ideal that anyone can overcome their personal problems of the past. Mark does more than just stand up to the bureaucracy; he uses the values he learned from basketball to fight for educational justice. I strongly recommend reading this brilliant story."

INTRODUCTION

This book, *They Call Me Pathfinder: Education—Basketball—Equality,* is a story of a young Jewish boy who grew up in his hometown of Worcester Massachusetts. My dad, Charlie Epstein, was my hero from the day I was born. I was not unlike many other young boys. I wanted to spend every waking second of every day with Dad. Charlie was an old-fashioned peddler who also owned a well-known sporting goods store that eventually I worked in as I got older.

I was lacking the maturity and motivation when it came to my academics. My dream of playing in the NBA was not unlike many other kids in Worcester during the 1960s. The Boston Celtics' dynasty was in full bloom and was being led by Bob Cousy, a Worcester resident from the same neighborhood I was growing up in. It was easy to want to be like "Mr. Basketball," as Bob Cousy was called in those days.

During my eighth-grade year, a school counselor recommended to my parents that I should receive a Boys' Trade education. It was during my days at Worcester Boys' Trade that I knew I was going to have lots of problems if I didn't get serious toward my schoolwork. I wanted to have a college education, which came about when I graduated from Worcester State College in 1975.

One day I picked up a book called *Black Like Me,* and from that day forward, I lived with a secret. My secret was living in the deep south and fighting for civil rights justices.

After suffering through a heartbreak with my first love and then a divorce with two young daughters, it was time to pack up and leave my family, friends, and hometown of Worcester.

My journey south was made up of intense determination as I settled into Charleston, South Carolina, and lived through even more drama and romance. It was time to find myself in a faraway place.

Using my Worcester State degree and my basketball background to open career doors, I started making a big impact in the Charleston County School District. It was time to live out my dream of being an agent for change in the Deep South.

A bachelor's life, a master's degree, a twenty-seven-year career in education, a coaching career, a marriage, and more adventures than I can even begin to remember are all included in this open and honest amazing journey. How this lost soul from Worcester, Massachusetts, found his way to a life in the Lowcountry of South Carolina that was once only read in a book became an American dream come true by using blind faith.

From desperation to receiving the MLK Award for the Lowcountry of South Carolina in 2016, "Pathfinder" has lived it all. Buckle in as Mark "Pathfinder" Epstein shares with you not only the magic of befriending some of the greatest athletes in American history but also the daily interactions of the students and their parents in the Deep South.

—Mark "Pathfinder" Epstein

FOREWORD

This is a true story of courage with integrity, and a dream that came true. I wrote this as a personal friend of Mark and his family.

Mark Epstein, aka "Pathfinder", is a 68-year-old Jewish white man who is remarried to Barbara Epstein, and together they have four children and seven grandchildren. Pathfinder grew up in a northern city called, Worcester, Massachusetts with his mom, dad, and three siblings. Mark was educated in the public-school system and has a bachelor's degree from Worcester State University. Pathfinder worked in the family clothing and sporting goods store with his father. Mark was active in all sports especially basketball and in sponsoring road races. His life was usual and typical.

Secretly, he had a dream – to emulate, in his own way, the person in a book entitled "Black Like Me", where a white man adds color to his skin and became a black person in the South.

In 1988, after a near death experience, Mark left his Worcester home and settled down in the Charleston, SC area. He finished his education with a master's degree from The Citadel and became a guidance counselor and athletic mentor in schools with mainly black students. His dream was coming true.

This book shows how he improved the lives of underprivileged students, especially to raise the school drop-out age from 17 to 18 and to help these immature kids to stay in school and know that the system would help.

Mark's relationship with named sports figures and politicians and how they also became involved, is exciting and enlightening.

This book is authentic and if you are fortunate, maybe you will meet Mark personally. As for me, I love him and admire this persistency in his goal of <u>EVERYONE'S LIFE MATTERS</u> and Mark is doing it "his way".

Sincerely:
Burton F. Berg – Attorney at Law, Worcester MA

One

BLACK LIKE ME

Ask anyone, and they'll tell you. There are some people and moments that have an impact on us all the way from childhood to adulthood. Sometimes it's a family member, coach, teacher, friend, or neighbor. Sometimes we don't even realize it until years later, as we mature. I've had a lot of positive influences. I've had lots of moments. It took me a long time to get serious toward my schoolwork, so to say that for me my key moment was a book shocks me still. I remember my favorite teacher of all time was Carol Konopka, whom I had when I was in fifth grade at May Street School, a middle-class neighborhood school in Worcester, Massachusetts. No way would I have ever thought I would have been impacted by a book. I'm still shocked I even read one in fifth grade.

You see, I was not your typical Jewish kid. I was not being driven toward a successful career that depended on academics. Nope, not for a second. I always thought I had a career in the NBA waiting for me. Yeah, I was your elementary school–age kid who couldn't find enough minutes in the day to play basketball. It didn't matter what time of day it was—the day of the week, the temperature, or anything else. I was convinced I had been put on this earth to play basketball. When I was in second grade, our family, which consisted of my older sister, Diane; my brother, Bobby; and my younger sister, Beth,

1

moved from Worcester's old Jewish neighborhood, called Vernon Hill to Worcester's West Side. Years later Diane became a huge influence in my life, especially when she graduated from college. I wanted what she had. Even now when I need a family member to talk with, Diane is my go-to. Bobby and I were given a full-size basketball court by our dad, Charlie Epstein (who was my hero from the second I was born—I'll get back to him later). Dad thought, what better way to attract friends in our new neighborhood than to build such a basketball court in a vacant lot given to him by a friendly neighbor. I was hooked immediately. How could kids growing up in Central Massachusetts in the late fifties and early sixties not get hooked on basketball?

Just like any other little brother, I looked up to my older brother, Bobby, whom we all called "Eppy". Eppy loved basketball even more than I did when we were growing up. He was rather good. He was a terrific shooter from the deep corners. He followed the NBA like it was his religion. Full-color photos of the NBA stars of our youth littered the walls of the bedroom we shared. He not only could recite every single player who played in the league from 1947 through the mid-1970s, but he could also tell you where each one went to college.

Every summer Dad sent Eppy and me to the Worcester Academy Sports Camp. This is where we met a lot of our lifelong friends. Coach Dee Rowe was the camp director. Coach Rowe had also built Worcester Academy into a New England prep school basketball powerhouse in the fifties and sixties. Later Coach Rowe left Worcester Academy and became the head coach at the University of Connecticut, where he had a lot of success. To this day Coach Rowe is a dear family friend.

Here is the interesting thing about Eppy. He hated the Celtics. He was a die-hard Lakers fan. He worshipped Jerry West and Elgin Baylor of the Lakers, both of whom are still considered two of the greatest players in basketball history.

He kept this secret to himself, though, unless you walked into our bedroom and saw the Lakers photos all over the walls. Years later I had the chance to work at a camp with Jerry West, and I put Jerry on the phone with Eppy. It was a nice experience for Bobby.

The Boston Celtics—led by the great Bill Russell and two Worcester residents, Bob Cousy and Tommy Heinsohn, who were both all-Americans at Holy Cross in Worcester—helped establish the team as one of America's great sports dynasties. Of course, we all wanted to be like the great "Mr. Basketball," as Bob Cousy was called.

Other influences that we had in our backyards were two of the most successful college basketball programs in America. Holy Cross was nationally recognized because it had won both the National Invitational Tournament (NIT) and the NCAA tournament several years earlier. Holy Cross was back on the upswing with George Blaney as the coach. Then there was Assumption College, whose team was ranked number one in division-two several years in a row. Assumption was being coached by Joe O'Brien, who was so dignified and polished he could have been a US Senator from Massachusetts.

The book! I have to get back to the book! I'm still in disbelief I was influenced by a book. I took the book home and hid it from my mom. My dad couldn't have cared less whether or not I did my homework. As it was getting closer to the book report deadline, I thought I'd read the first couple of pages and bluff my way through the book report. I read the first two pages, and, to my shock, I thought, *Not bad.* I decided to keep reading until I got bored and then turn the book back in. I never got bored. I kept reading. I was in total disbelief. I finished it and wanted to keep reading it. I never turned it back in. John Howard Griffin had entered my life. Until now I have never told a single person that I wanted to be John Howard Griffin. Being Cousy would have been awesome, but being like John Howard Griffin was even better. I wanted to paint myself black and travel throughout the Deep South and experience racial segregation. *Black Like Me* by John Howard Griffin became my tucked-away Bible.

Worcester is a city of about two hundred thousand people located in the very heart of Massachusetts. It is known primarily as a large blue-collar manufacturing hub. In its heyday some of the largest manufacturers in the world called Worcester home. Unfortunately, the economy's recession in the first decade of the twenty-first century brought Worcester to its knees. Recently, though, my wonderful hometown has been undergoing a huge rebirth. People from all over are moving in, and new businesses have started popping up. In fact, the Boston Red Sox AAA affiliate has left Rhode Island and will be moving into their brand-new stadium on the grounds where the manufacturing giant Wyman-Gordon used to be.

Oh, the charm of my hometown! How I miss it! No city in America will ever come close to its old-style three-deckers, which now have a more modern look. It's the neighborhoods that made Worcester so special for its longtime residents, though. What awesome neighborhoods! Drive through Shrewsbury Street and you'll find the old-school Italians. In the Vernon Hill area are many Irish residents. Main-South has a large Latin population. Go to the Island District, and you've got old-school Polish. The West Side has become home to the Jewish community. African American residents are scattered among all these neighborhoods.

Like any urban city in America, Worcester has gone through some changes in the last few years. There has become a larger diverse population that has moved in, and this has changed the close-knit neighborhoods and the old-fashioned camaraderie a little bit. When I was growing up though, there was no better city in America I would have rather lived in. It didn't hurt that Boston was only forty miles to the east.

I was a pretty weak student growing up. I just didn't have the motivation to succeed. I still regret my lack of direction. Fortunately, I found it just before it might have been too late.

After struggling through my early years in school, it was recommended by my eighth-grade guidance counselor that I attend Worcester Boys' Trade. I still do not understand why he made this recommendation. For me this was the wrong placement. Before students entered Trade, each had to select the top two shop majors they wanted to study. My first choice was electrical work. Not being sure what I wanted my second choice to be, I chose printing. I do not know why. Much to my disappointment, I was placed in the printing program. On the first day of my freshman year, I inquired about changing my shop placement. I did not know it at the time, but Trade had a strict policy that would not allow students to change majors. If I had decided to transfer to my home high school after my freshman year, I would have been required to start ninth grade all over again. For the next four years, I was in no-man's-land.

What I never could have imagined was during my junior and senior years I was going to become the victim of the meanest and cruelest type of terrorism a student can suffer through. It was a combination of anti-Semitism and harassment. It was only a small group of students. My high school basketball teammates and the faculty were all terrific. During the last month of my senior year, I finally told my next-door neighbor Don Lemenager what I had been dealing with. Don was the basketball coach and athletic director at Trade, and later he became my lifetime friend and mentor. He felt awful. I had kept everything to myself. It was tough.

Let me clarify something. No one will ever have more respect than I do for the need to offer young people career-training opportunities. I saw firsthand how much Boys' Trade did for so many of my classmates. Not only have they had successful careers, but they have also added so much to the needed workforce over the years in Worcester County.

During my last couple of years in high school, I realized I wanted to receive a college education. I studied independently for my college boards by buying an SAT study guide. Trade did not offer the core curriculum that was being offered at traditional high schools.

Unfortunately, I had fallen even further behind in my academics. I did well enough on my SAT to receive a provisional acceptance into Worcester State University in my hometown. This was my big break! I was determined not to screw it up.

Before I could get a full acceptance into Worcester State, I had to take two college-level courses at a local two-year community college. I had to receive Bs in both a college algebra class and a college-level English literature class. I thought for sure I was in over my head. Much to my surprise, I received the Bs I needed. I still had one more hoop to jump through before I could start taking classes at WSU. I had to attend a six-week summer program four days per week for orientation into a full college academic curriculum. I also had to show the professors that I had made sufficient progress within the summer program. Only ten students were in the program, and all ten were given full acceptance at the end of the summer.

My whole family was overjoyed with the progress I was making. I knew it was way too early to celebrate anything. I had a long way to go to make it to my main goal, which was graduating from college and receiving a bachelor's degree.

My biggest hurdles were learning how to manage my severe case of ADHD and studying. I enjoyed being a college student and finally getting a chance to carry books around campus. I was on top of the world. At Trade students had been required to leave the books we were given to use in the classroom for the next group of students. The other part of college I enjoyed was going to school with girls. Boys' Trade did not allow girls when I attended.

I knew what my strengths and weaknesses were, so to compensate for my ADHD, I became hyper-focused. I must have driven my professors and other students crazy. I never stopped asking questions in class. I found the library and was excited. During my years at Trade, there had been no library.

What I especially wanted to do was play college basketball. There was not a day that went by from third grade on that you wouldn't find me playing basketball at the Worcester Jewish Community Center or on the family court my dad had built. There were two problems I had when it came to playing at WSU. I did not know whether I was good enough, and I was not sure it was a good idea. I feared that even if I did make the team, it might become a distraction from my real purpose of going to college.

I had taken a year off between Trade and WSU. I had enlisted in the Massachusetts National Guard during my senior year of high school and had had to fulfill my five months of basic training in New Jersey.

Basketball was in my blood. My body was so weak and frail I had not come close to my potential yet. I knew the game as well as anyone could, but I was a couple of years away from my body gaining the strength needed to play on the college level.

My basketball mentors were both first team all-Americans at Holy Cross. Togo Palazzi and Jack "The Shot'" Foley remain true legends. Each got drafted by the Celtics eight years apart. "The Shot" was my high school coach at Trade for four years. Jack is still considered one of the greatest college basketball shooters in NCAA Division I history. He attended high school at Assumption Prep in Worcester. In three varsity seasons at Holy Cross, Jack scored over twenty-two hundred points. All three seasons Foley's teams made the postseason NIT played at Madison Square Garden in New York City. Holy Cross won five games during those three seasons in the NIT. During Jack's senior season, he averaged close to thirty-four points per game. He finished his career with an over twenty-seven-point average. The only reason his NBA career was so short was that his body was too skinny to take the physical pounding that playing in the NBA required.

The funniest thing about Jack was he was a collector of snakes. He knew I was petrified of them. One night while in college, I stayed over at his house. He told me he had left a towel out for me to use when I showered. Just as I was ready to go into the shower, I looked down and, to my total shock, there were three large boa constrictors staring at me. Oh, my goodness—I'm still having nightmares. Jack made me feel a lot better, though. As he was falling over laughing, he said, "Don't worry, Pathfinder, most nights they stay in the bathroom."

Let me say these final words about my guy Jack Foley. They do not call him "The Shot" for nothing. Both Togo and Jack remain two of the very closest friends I have ever had. I met Togo when I was seven and have referred to him as "Uncle" Togo throughout my life. Togo was the MVP of the NIT when he led Holy Cross to the NIT championship his senior year. I still talk once a week to Uncle Togo. Togo is eighty-eight now, with failing health. It is going to be a sad day when

Togo is not there to tell me any more stories of his career playing for the legendary Boston Celtics.

A wonderful friendship developed during the winter months after I returned home from New Jersey. I found myself playing basketball all over Worcester to keep in shape. One day I found myself playing against Jimmy McGovern from Holy Name High, also in Worcester. Jimmy would go on to become the closest friend I had ever had at that time. Mac (as he was called by his friends) was a senior in high school. He had not decided what college he would attend or whether he was interested in playing basketball beyond high school.

I decided I just had to recruit Mac to also attend WSU and play basketball, so one day we could possibly become college teammates. The first of many recruitments during my life was a success. Mac did attend WSU, and we became inseparable over the next twenty years. Not only did we become close, but our two families also became one. Mac's sister, Marian, whom I still refer to as "Lil Sis," became the top colonel for the Massachusetts State Police. If you don't think Mac and I were given several lectures on our behavior, oh man—were we scared of screwing up!

There was only one problem I did not realize at the time with Mac joining me at Worcester State. Mac was terrific and received lots more playing time than I did. I still say that Mac might have been the most underrated player that ever played for the Lancers. He was the point guard and defensive glue that kept all the egos happy by making sure our big scorers got the ball when they were open. Forget the four points per game he averaged; we would not have been as successful and have gone to the school's first national postseason tournament our junior year without him. To this day we still laugh about the turn of events. My big recruit—and I sat and watched him.

My freshman year I struggled academically, which was not a big surprise to anyone. My sophomore year was a much different story, though. During the second semester of my sophomore year, I shocked the world and made the honor roll.

I did try out at WSU; I think the coaches caught a glimpse of my love for the game and my potential. I played JV my first year and a half, as my size and strength were still playing catch-up. During my final two years I played on the varsity. It remains a thrill for me that even though I never got the playing time I was hoping for, I was part of the best basketball era (1971–1974) in WSU history.

It would have been hard for the WSU Lancers not to have been good during those years. The Lancers had some big-time players who could have played for any major university in the country. Malcolm "Big Dog" Person and Sonny "Little Dog" Price combined to score fifty points per game between them, and each became all-Americans for their play during the 1973–1974 season. Malcolm was originally from Alabama, and later his two nephews had brilliant, long careers in the NBA. Their names are Chuck and Wesley Person. They combined to score over twenty-two thousand points between them during their NBA careers. It was in their bloodline.

There were many faculty members who still stand out to me. There was one I took a special liking to. Joe Tracy came to WSU for only my senior year. He had just left the priesthood and was a newlywed. He taught sociology. His classes were a blast. We became close friends, and we spent a lot of time together outside of campus after I graduated. Joe was not rehired because of the budget. He was at WSU for only one year and then gone. I often wonder what became of my favorite professor.

My four years in college flew by. During my senior year, I met a beautiful young coed student whom I quickly developed strong feelings for. This young lady, who was both beautiful and sweet, became my first steady girlfriend. We stayed together for three years, and we were married for a year and a half before we both decided to go our own way. A few months ago, we met for the first time in over forty years and enjoyed some fun memories we share from when we were much younger. We both feel awful that neither one of us was ready for marriage. I know I have never uttered a single negative word about my first love, and she has said the same. I believe her. Facebook can be a wonderful thing.

* * *

If we had the chance to do it all again
Tell me, would we? Could we?
—Barbra Streisand, "The Way We Were"

Time to graduate! Who could have imagined I would earn a bachelor's degree in four years? Better yet, who could have imagined I would graduate with a double major in psychology and elementary education? Not I.

Without a doubt my bachelor's degree will always remain my greatest accomplishment. I had never felt such pride. Also, I had never had to work so hard to try to accomplish something.

I owe so much to my mom, Sarah Epstein. Her steadfast love, support, and encouragement were critical for me. Mom knew when I needed a push, and she knew when I needed a cheerleader. Those qualities really became important to me later in life, as you will read about later in this book. I was now a graduate of Worcester State University! Go, Fighting Lancers!

Two

Pathfinder

I knew what I was going to do for a career before I attended college, but I still did not want to miss out on a college education. Charlie's Surplus and Athletic Equipment on Water Street in Worcester was a family-run business owned by my dad, Charlie Epstein. Oh, what a tremendous man. I have always been overwhelmed with pride and joy, since the day I was born, to have Charles Epstein as my father. I never tried to hide it, and it became immediately evident to everyone when my father and I were together.

My sister Diane was convinced I had a serious language deficit when I was a child. Diane would constantly tell my mom to take me to a doctor to have me checked out. I walked around all day until I was over four years old repeating the same sentence, "I want to go Daddy car." My mom kept telling my sister that if I could say those five words, eventually I was going to be able to add a few more to my arsenal. I must admit, though, I was driving everyone nuts.

Charlie's Surplus was located on Water Street in Worcester, which has been a stronghold of Jewish businesses dating back all the way to the migration period of Jews coming over from Europe to Massachusetts. Starting from when I was three years old, Dad would take to me to his store, a warehouse about the size of a small bedroom. Dad loved having an image for Charlie's Surplus as a surplus rummage sale. Boxes were piled on top of each other, and rubber bands were used to keep all the shoes and sneakers together as pairs. Charlie felt that, with an image of low overhead, people would think they were getting a huge savings with every purchase made. A lot of times this wasn't the case. Nothing was priced, so if he thought a customer really wanted an item, he would charge a little more. As I write this story, I find myself laughing at this fact.

Dad grew up as the next-to-the-next-to-the-youngest of six children in a poor Jewish family that had settled in Worcester. His parents had emigrated from Lithuania at the turn of the twentieth century. Dad was not much of a student. After he was done with high school, he joined the Civil Corps (CC) camp in the western part of Massachusetts. The CC camps were set up by the US government to offer jobs to young men during the Depression years preceding World War II.

Dad loved sports. He loved baseball. When I was growing up, his friends all used to tell me about what a tremendous slugger he had been. I did see this also. When we were young, every Sunday afternoon Dad would take my brother and me and all our friends from our neighborhood to a baseball field, where we would play sandlot games all day long.

His favorite sports, though, were boxing and bodybuilding. He claims he was one of Worcester's first bodybuilders. During his youth gyms were not set up with the equipment that they have today.

Tough! Oh, my! Words will never be able to explain how tough my dad was. I have tried for years. I do not come close. When my dad was young, if any Jewish person was being bullied with anti-Semitism, they would get Charlie, and that would be the end of any further teasing forever.

Once Dad enlisted in the Navy during World War II, he boxed his way to a top-ten ranking among all middleweight boxers in the US Navy. Now I think I am explaining how tough my dad was. Dad, as tough as he was, is still remembered in all New England as one of the most loving, kind, generous, and wonderful human beings who ever walked the planet. I told you I was proud to be Charlie Epstein's son.

12

My dad called himself a peddler. He was honored to call himself a peddler. Regardless of how much success he had, how much money he made, and who had become his closest friends, he wanted all his four children to tell people that he was a peddler, not a businessman. Dad was wired differently.

Right after the war, Dad came back to Worcester and married his "Sandy." It was at that time he decided to become a peddler. Off he went, carrying a suitcase on his back all over the countryside of Central Massachusetts. Dad could not yet afford a car, so every day he would carry his suitcase of forty pounds on his shoulder and hitchhike to every farmhouse in the "country," as he called it. He would not return home most nights until two or three o'clock in the morning.

"No days off" is a theme used often in today's workplace. I will bet any amount of money that quote was first used to describe Charlie Epstein. His farmer friends, as dad referred to them, would become members of his family as he would stop by for weekly visits for over fifty years.

Charlie knew every back road and every farmer in every small town in Worcester County. Every day of the week was a different route. Each Tuesday would be the Brookfields; each Wednesday would be Barre and Rutland; Thursdays would be Gilbertville and Old Furnace; Paxton and Oakham would be Fridays; Saturdays were stops in Ware. Dad became "Uncle Charlie" to almost every son and daughter as well as to grandchildren born to his longtime farmer friends.

I loved it when Dad would take me peddling with him. It was a blast. He drove a van that had a roof rack on top to carry his goods. The second we turned from our street, away from our home, he would pull over, and I would jump up on top of the rack and drive all day and night yelling down at him. There was only one rule that had to be followed. I was sworn to secrecy to not say a word about what we were doing to my mom. I am sure she knew, though, because every time we drove off, she would yell out the door that she didn't want me riding on the roof rack.

Dad eventually moved from his small warehouse to further up Water Street, closer to all the hustle and bustle of the bakeries, kosher butchers, fruit stores, kosher delis, drugstore, bar, and supermarket. I can still remember him picking me up after school when I was in fifth grade to show me his new store. We were all so proud of him.

What is important to know is my dad did not have any favorites among his four children. Also, every one of my siblings felt the exact same way about Dad. I had no different feelings about him than my brother and sisters did.

Dad had a funny way of making sure everyone he knew had a special nickname. My sister Diane was Daylight, Beth was Afternoon, my brother, Bobby, was Eppy. All our friends were called by their first names along with the last letter of their last name. For a short time, he gave himself the nickname Trailblazer. I was Pathfinder from the time I was twelve years old. No, I was never a Cub Scout, Boy Scout, Eagle Scout, or even a Brownie. I was named after the Pathfinder sleeping bags that were being sold at Charlie's Surplus. My mom was even given the name Mount Everest, for about a day.

My nickname was the only one that was leaked outside of the family, and it was the only one that stuck. I guarantee there are some people who have known me for the last fifty years who do not know my real first name is Mark. I love it. Once in a rare instance when my closest friends refer to me as Mark, I politely correct them and ask them to call me Pathfinder. In a way I think the nickname kind of fits me well. My family and friends think so also.

Charlie Epstein did an amazing job building his family business. In his own way, he was brilliant. Forget about business classes; this guy could have been a professor at Harvard Business School. The best words to describe his business style are *unconventional* and *old school*. I learned more about business, life, promoting, marketing, and buying than I could have from any college professor.

His lessons served me far better than my college education later in life, when I moved away and started my work in the Charleston (South Carolina) County School District. The biggest lesson I learned was, get out in the community and market yourself. If you do it right and use all the means available, you will be successful in everything you do. Dad was like the ringleader of the Barnum & Bailey Circus.

We became an extraordinarily successful team. The team also consisted of several others. I use the word "team," but it was much more like a close-knit family. I loved my coworkers. We all did everything together outside of work. Everyone was into sports, especially basketball and baseball. We had George Query, who had started with my dad when he was twelve years old. Then there were the two St. Mary's High buddies, Dave Meehan, and Bob Kusz. One of the saddest moments of my life was when Dave was killed after work trying to break up a fight. It is still so sad for so many. We had other coworkers who were phenomenal people. Sophia Barsham was from Turkey, and Kathy Shannon Fitzpatrick was from nearby Grafton. Those were the full-time staff members. So many other athletes, such as Holy Cross basketball star Jim McCaffrey from Vermont, who became one of my closest friends and still is, and former Fairfield basketball player Dave Bradley from Worcester, along with many others would come and go on a part-time basis.

Dad loved to sponsor both youth and adult sports teams. It did not matter what it was. Football, soccer, little league, softball—you name it. Dad loved knowing everyone had an opportunity to participate in healthy living. In fact, Dad and his best childhood friend, Paul Tivnan, who was the director of the Worcester Parks Department, started the first women's summer basketball league in Massachusetts back in 1973.

Charlie's Surplus became well-known throughout all New England because of Dad and basketball. He entered his family business into one of the finest semipro summer basketball leagues on the East Coast. Worcester Park's Summer League had many of the fiercest rivalries I have ever been involved with. Almost immediately Charlie's Surplus became dominant. Our players remain some of the greatest legendary college and professional players in New England history. The regional local paper, *The Worcester Telegram and Gazette*, had a full-time staff member assigned to cover all the games. This was a huge benefit for all the sponsors. If you won, you would get huge free publicity. It surely did not hurt the business of Charlie's Surplus. Crowds of up to two to three thousand fans would line the court and sit on a big hill overlooking Cousy Court on any given evening.

Dad got me involved in putting our teams together and in coaching them. Over a nine-year period, we won seven championships. We had it going. We were not the most popular because a lot of our players came from both the Boston area and Connecticut. Another reason we were not exceedingly popular was because of me. I wanted to win and never stop. I think as a team we were extremely cocky, but my brother and dad thought I was the cockiest. I just wanted to win so badly. I was finally achieving the success I desperately had wanted as a player.

The funny part of this for me remains the fact that during the first couple of years, I would put our Charlie's team together and play for the deli located next door, Tom's Meat Mart. Tom's was being coached by my high school coach, Jack "The Shot" Foley. He knew I was not good enough to play on Charlie's, but he also had followed me carefully and knew I was a late bloomer and had become a pretty good scorer. The other nice thing about hooking up with Tom's was it gave me a chance to play again with my boy Timmy Ethier, whom I had played with at WSU.

I had been playing so much that if we had put my high school team back together, I felt I might have been the best player. In fact, some of my high school teammates from Trade who had entered their working careers and had not seen me play for a few years were shocked to see how much I had improved years later. It's all about strength, continuing to work, and confidence. Being a good player, though, is all relative to the competition you're playing against. I could go to the Jewish Community Center and be a very good player and then go to WSU and fight for playing time. When I left WSU, my coach told me that if I had been six-foot-five, I would have been an all-American. I laughed. I didn't know what he meant then, and I'm still confused now because I'm only six-foot-one. The point is I became very competitive and I felt I could compete with just about anyone.

A good example of a late bloomer is a good buddy, Jim Burke from UMass. Jim received a scholarship offer from UMass only after Julius Erving left after his junior year to sign a lucrative pro contract. That's right, Jim Burke remains the answer to a historic basketball trivia question. Ask anyone who took Dr. J's scholarship when he left U-Mass early, and if they answer "Jim Burke," I will give you a million dollars! Jim spent his entire career as an exceptionally good role player on some of the best teams in U-Mass history. In fact, Jim was the captain his senior year when U-Mass received its fifth NIT invitation in six years.

Once Jim left U-Mass, his game exploded. I wasn't even sure I wanted him on our team. The only reason he was, is because his teammate at U-Mass was six-foot-nine John Murphy, who had just received the Yankee Conference Player of The Year his senior year. John had just been drafted by the Chicago Bulls and told me if his best friend Jim Burke wasn't going to play, he wasn't either. That situation was quickly cleared up. It's worth noting that throughout Charlie's Surplus's entire tenure playing in the league, over twenty of our players were NBA draft picks. Not counting another five who were all-Americans and many others who played professionally in Europe. I think you're starting to understand that Charlie's Surplus was loaded.

My dad, my brother, and I usually didn't agree on many things when it came to basketball. But if you asked any of us who the best player we ever had was, without hesitating we would name Jim Burke. Here was a guy who had his highest point average of six points his senior season, but who had the most athletic ability I had ever seen play at Crompton Park, where all the games were played. Late bloomers happen. Jim went on to play in Germany for a couple of years and led his team to the German championship, averaging thirty points per game. If he came out of college now, he would have a ten-year NBA career waiting for him. Another thing about my guy "Burkie", as we all called him, was that he was offered a tryout with the Dallas Cowboys in the seventies as a defensive back. It was during the great Roger Staubach years, and Jim Burke had never even played football. His U-Mass coach, the legendary Jack Lehman, once told me Jim Burke was the second-best athlete that he had coached during his thirteen seasons at U-Mass. I nearly fell over. Coach Lehman did not have to remind me for a second that he had also coached the legendary Dr. J. The guy was an athletic freak who had suddenly become confident in his abilities.

My favorite Charlie's player of all time was Owen Mahorn from Hartford, Connecticut, an alumnus of Weaver High and Fairfield University. What a legend! What a great guy, and what a brother he became to me! When Owen died a few years ago, I left work early and sat in a park near where I was working in Charleston, South Carolina, during Owen's funeral. Owen would bring his younger brother, who was in high school, with him whenever we had a game. We gave his little brother a team jersey and put him on the roster. Well, the little brother did not stay little for too long. Rick Mahorn went on to become the mastermind of the Detroit Pistons "Bad Boy" teams of the late eighties, which were led by Isiah Thomas. Those Piston teams won back-to-back NBA championships. I hate to spoil this exciting story about NBA legend Rick Mahorn, but Owen Mahorn was far and away the best player in the Mahorn family.

Lastly, when someone years later asked how good our teams were, I answered this way: good enough for three to four years to take a Big East schedule, win twenty games, and get an invite to play in the NCAA tournament.

* * *

Charlie's Surplus was starting to establish itself in the retail and wholesale business. Dad was a masterful buyer. He knew how to find incredible deals that most store owners would walk away from. He was also a tough negotiator. Once there was an agreement, though, he was a man of his word.

Dad wanted to have the image in his store of a low-end discount shop. There were no thrills and not even a cash register. Everything went straight into the pocket. There were receipts given out, but Charlie trusted his help.

It was at about the time I was working at Charlie's on weekends that I discovered how comfortable I was around our Black customers. Maybe it was part of my basketball background and the many Black friendships I had formed. We were not raised with any prejudice toward anyone. Neither Mom nor Dad would have tolerated any of that nonsense from any of their children.

Everyone came from far and wide to buy their reject Converse Chuck Taylors at less than half price. You could find work shoes, Doc Martens, jackets, jeans, team athletic uniforms, socks, and sweats of all styles and colors. We had a screen-printing T-shirt business going also. Sidewalk sales were popular at Charlie's. If Dad wanted to get rid of some old merchandise, out on the sidewalk it went. Peacoats, army jackets, army pants, windbreakers, and ball caps would all disappear off the shelves as quickly as we could restock them. Saucony running shoes and Spot-Bilt athletic shoes at discounted prices were a rage. Of course, we sold camping equipment. It's a shame those Pathfinder sleeping bags were such slow movers.

Charlie's had several floors of warehouse space above the store and further down on Water Street that were out of view. What very few besides the workers knew was that we were supplying several of the local manufacturers around New England their industrial safety supplies and work clothing. We had some accounts that were purchasing several hundred dozen work gloves at a time a couple of times a week. Charlie was incredible at being the underdog salesman and walking away with accounts that would bring in thousands. He taught me well. Several times a year, I would "hit the road" and work my Charlie Epstein magic on company buyers; it would work well at times. There was no need to feel sorry for my dad the peddler. I was bursting with pride over his success.

Do not get me wrong—we had our clashes, like any father and son who were extremely close and working together would. There were times our personalities would clash over the image of the store. I wanted a more up-to-date look, and my dad wanted it to look like it was a rummage sale. At times I wanted to open accounts with Nike and Adidas, but Dad wasn't interested because they didn't offer close-outs and rejects at reduced prices. I understood because what we had going was working well. I was concerned, though, about the future because I had remarried, and my children were little.

I'll tell you what else Dad was a master at. He put together some of the world's funniest ads in our regional paper, *The Worcester Telegram and Gazette.* In the winter months, we sold ice skates. I mean thousands of ice skates at incredible savings. He would place ads in the paper with photos of our workers describing them as famous figure skaters or hockey players. No one who ever worked at Charlie's had even walked on ice. He would place an ad that would describe made-up accomplishments. He would tell how Sophia had been a silver medalist in the Calgary Winter Olympics. He would describe Bobby Kusz as a top prospect with the New York Rangers who knew how to offer tips on fitting hockey skates. He described Dave Meehan as the greatest men's figure skater in the world until he fell and hurt his knee. He had a photo of me with a basketball in my hand captioned "Shop at Charlie's for Your Converse Sneakers, and Let Pathfinder Fit You." He had in the ad that I had played two and a half games for the Atlanta Hawks and had been cut at halftime. Shockingly, some people thought I *had* played for the Hawks. But the best ad I have ever seen in my life was a cartoon of my mom, Sarah Epstein, on skates. He described her as a gold medal favorite in women's speed skating at the 1948 Olympics in Switzerland. Dad had written above the cartoon in the ad that Mom had given up a promising career on the ice to have a family instead. Oh, my goodness! You should have seen my mom's face the first time she came into the store and saw her ad up on the wall. I had to go home, and I did not return that day because I had never laughed so hard in my life.

What I have always admired most about my dad is the fact that he considered himself a peddler first. He would still go out in his van five nights a week stopping at farmhouses all over Massachusetts, visiting and selling whatever he had to his lifelong farmer friends.

His most famous stop of all time was in North Brookfield one night at his buddy Gil Markel's Longview Farm. Gil owned a world-renowned recording studio on his farm, where famous music groups would rehearse for a few weeks before going on tour. Dad stopped late one night, and a few strangers approached his van as he was pulling out his boxes to show Gil. One stranger took a box and brought it into the studio without asking. Charlie freaked out. He started hollering for his friend Gil to come out. Gil asked Dad what was wrong. Dad replied, "Some kook just stole a box of work shoes from me."

Gil said, "Charlie, that's not a kook; that's Mick Jagger from the Rolling Stones."

Charlie Epstein, on cue, like the master peddler he was, yelled out, "Hey, Mick. Come on back; I gave you the wrong box. Those are the low-end shoes; this box has the much-better-quality ones that you'll like even more."

I guarantee you one thing: Mick Jagger's boots shot up from forty dollars to four thousand dollars in a matter of six-tenths of a second.

People—my wife Barbara among them—are always saying my mind of ideas never stops spinning. While working later in my career in education in South Carolina, I was always coming up with new programs and ideas that no one in our school district had ever thought of. Whenever I came up with a new concept that I thought had a chance to help the students, I would always try and sell it to the local media to help promote it. I am sure some in the local media thought of me as a grandstander; how could they not? But what they didn't know about was my background in business with my dad Charlie Epstein at Charlie's Surplus. How could I not be wired differently? I had learned from the master.

Dad loved sports. He loved organizing and promoting. In 1976 the country was getting ready for its huge bicentennial celebration. He wanted to do something special for his hometown of Worcester. He had this romance with running, especially running long distances.

Every Patriot's Day in April we would go to the world-famous Boston Marathon, where we would stay and pass out water until the last runners made their way across the finish line. We both loved it. We were both hooked on marathon running.

One day we were talking, and he said, "Let's start a long-distance race for the people of Central Mass." I liked the idea, but I reminded him we knew absolutely nothing about organizing a road race. He told me we didn't need to know anything. He suggested we recruit a couple of local high school track coaches who did. So just like that the world-famous Annual Charlie's Surplus Ten-Mile Road Race was hatched. Off we went, putting together a committee of over one hundred members. Some were outstanding runners from their high school and college days, and some needed help walking to the bathroom. It didn't matter. If Charlie asked, you couldn't say no.

We chose to hold the event in the afternoon on Mother's Day. We weren't sure of the course, but Dad told members of the committee that he wanted the course set for ten miles on the West Side of Worcester with the finish line at historic Elm Park, which is the second oldest public park in America.

Now, here was the thing about having the race on Mother's Day. Lots of people voiced concerns that it interfered with their dinner plans. Others complained that there were roads being blocked and they could not get to where they needed to go. Both were legitimate concerns. Dad and I felt it was an advantage to use Mother's Day, and here is the reason why: Many runners from out of town would put aside that day to come to Worcester and visit with their families. They were able to run and have their families join in the festivities at the finish line at Elm Park, where the race ended. Families could also line the course and cheer on their favorite runners.

Charlie's Race attracted runners from seventeen states one year, and for a Worcester race, that is a huge number. On a nice spring day there were as many as fifteen to twenty thousand fans lining the course. Entire families of all ages would cheer, throw water, and stay for the entire afternoon. Best of all there was still plenty of time for those dinner reservations for celebrations. Racing ten miles is not easy, and it gave everyone something to talk about over dinner. Charlie's Race became not only a family event but also a huge community party to celebrate the beginning of spring.

Charlie and I started working hard to get the word out. We met with our local media, who absolutely loved the idea. The running boom was just starting to take off around the country. On weekends we would drive around to races and hand out leaflets and race applications and invite everyone we met to come to Worcester and race on Mother's Day.

We got our first of the many huge breaks we would get over the next ten years. The winner of the Boston Marathon the year before was becoming a megastar in the world of sports in America. His name was Bill Rodgers. Bill had just announced he would not be defending his championship from the previous year. The Boston Marathon committee was tremendously disappointed and made a big deal about it. Bill was training for the Olympic trials that were going to be held on May 25. Bill didn't want to take a chance on burning himself out and hurting his chances of representing the United States in the Olympic Games in Montreal later that summer.

Bill was from Connecticut and was already creating a huge local following all over New England. Dad had heard that Bill's new in-laws lived in Worcester. Our brains were spinning. I said, "Dad, let's try and get ahold of Bill and invite him to stop by the store and win him over." A few days later, Bill and his wife and in-laws came in, and we walked to the back of the store. I talked first about how a ten-mile race could be used for a tune-up two weeks before the biggest marathon of his life. Charlie made a pitch. "You can make this a big family celebration on Mother's Day by coming to Worcester and racing in front of your new in-laws."

We had our guy! Bill Rodgers was in. We had our press conference at the store. In a short time, the Boston media picked up the news, and we were being talked about all over New England. How could the defending Boston Marathon champion pass up returning and racing in Worcester at the Charlie's Surplus Ten-Mile Road Race that no one had ever heard of? Priceless!

The bicentennial in Worcester was great fun. On that beautiful spring afternoon, 350 runners showed up at the starting line in front of Doherty High School. Several of us had never run in a race, never mind racing ten miles. I was one of them. I laced up my high-top Converse Chuck Taylors, and away I sprinted. Ouch! Not a good idea.

Bill Rodgers was the first to cross the finish line at Elm Park about one hundred yards in front of the second-place racer. We had the winner we wanted. I came in who knows where. I did not stop, and I was not last, and that was all I cared about that day.

I think I need to get back to the Chuck Taylors I was wearing. I caught up with Bill at Elm Park about thirty minutes after he had crossed the finish line. The first thing he said when he saw me was, "Pathfinder, did you race in those high tops?"

I looked at him with a puzzled look and said, "You mean I should have raced in a low pair?"

Bill then asked me what size feet I had. I told him a size thirteen. Wouldn't you know it, but five days later a box of my very own pair of brand-new, size thirteen New Balance shoes arrived in the mail. They were so beautiful to me I did not want to wear them and get them dirty.

Charlie's Surplus Ten-Mile Road Race became more than anyone could have ever envisioned. Charlie was way ahead of his time. We caught the perfect storm at the perfect time. Talk about beating the boom. We established my dad's race just before the running boom of the seventies and eighties hit full force. Dad, several committee members, and I worked around the calendar to make sure the race stayed on everyone's mind twelve months a year.

During the second edition of Charlie's in 1977, Bill Rodgers was no longer a national celebrity. He was a worldwide phenomenon. Even though he didn't win a medal at the Olympics in Montreal in 1976, he was ranked as the number one marathon runner in the world. In fact, it would be seven years and twenty-two worldwide marathon victories later that he would give up his number one ranking.

Having "Boston Billy" (which was now what everyone was calling him) back had all the sports fans in Central Mass supercharged. The second edition doubled the number of runners to seven hundred. The media coverage was amazing for a small, family-owned surplus business. Even now when I'm writing this book and looking back at certain accomplishments of my dad's, I have to shake my head and laugh. The guy was that good. He never ceased to amaze me.

I know everyone loves their dad in a special way. I get that, absolutely. I have never ever said mine was more special, and I never will. You will have to search this earth for many a moon to find a more loyal son. That I will go to my grave knowing.

Bill Rodgers won again. Perfect! The sport of running was starting to change, with appearance money being given out by race sponsors. I felt even if "Boston Billy" could not return in 1978, we could use his name as a two-time Charlie's Surplus Road Race champion. That is a nice promotional vehicle to have. Do not think for one second that we did not take advantage of that. That is exactly what happened. Billy has stayed a good friend to this day. I love the guy.

In 1978 it had become common knowledge that amateurism in road racing was slowly coming to an end. Dad gave to me the responsibility of keeping alive the tradition of Charlie's Race being one of the top road races in New England. That meant recruiting elite athletes to compete with a limited budget. We were going to be put to the test.

We as a race committee stepped up our game. I was out hustling for every elite runner all over America. I figured if we were going to stay in the business of road racing, we needed to do it in a big way. I wasn't saying too much to anyone, including Charlie, but I didn't want just a popular New England road race. I wanted something much bigger.

The year 1978 was the first one in which we had women who were being recognized nationally. Randy Thomas, a prodigy of Rodgers from nearby Fitchburg, captured the first of his two Charlie's championships. Lynn Jennings was a phenomenon. She was a high school girl from Massachusetts whom everyone knew about. I wanted her badly. Lynn was dominant. Later, she won a bronze medal in the 1992 Olympics in Barcelona. She was absolutely crushing not only the women's competition but the men's as well. Before her career was through, Lynn had competed in three Olympic Games for Team USA and won four World Athletics Cross Country Championships. Lynn Jennings was that good.

As excited as I was to land Lynn, it was the second-place women's finisher that I had my eye on. Sharon Barbano was working as a counselor and track coach at Becker Junior College in Worcester. I was single at the time, and she had ordered some track uniforms from me. We hit it off and began training together. I knew before Sharon did that; she had the potential to be a national-class runner. Sharon Barbano has gone on to become a huge success in the running world. She has a couple of worldwide marathon championships to her credit, along with a slew of road race victories. She has competed in the US women's Olympic trials in the marathon. Later, Sharon became the spokeswoman for the L'eggs Road Race circuit for women. Sharon has been the VP of marketing and public relations for Saucony running shoes and apparel for many years. If you tune into the Boston Marathon, you will hear Sharon Barbano doing the live color on WBZ-TV in Boston. To say I am still proud of Sharon is an understatement. She has remained a wonderful friend, and I am happy to say she has never forgotten her humble beginnings. A world-class act Sharon is.

I am not going to break down every one of Charlie's Surplus Road Races. During our several years of sponsoring, we had the who's who of elite racers. In total we had seven Olympians representing three countries, seven Boston Marathon champions, several world record holders in various distances, another twenty-two runners who had won marathons all over the world, and more than fifty runners who had at least one road race during their careers.

Charlie's Surplus Ten-Mile Road Race peaked at close to two thousand runners in 1985 before Dad could no longer afford to sponsor it. The race continued for another ten years because the

Worcester Telegram and Gazette decided to take over the sponsorship. Even though Charlie's Race had a new title sponsor, the race to this day is remembered as Charlie's Surplus Ten-Mile Road Race.

If I had to select the absolute best elite athletes, we ever had race, they would be the following. Among the men, Bill Rodgers (four Boston Marathon wins and four New York City Marathon wins to his credit), Geoff Smith (two Boston Marathon victories and two Olympics appearances for Great Britain), Greg Meyer, Bob Hodge, Peter Pfitzinger, Bob Doyle, Randy Thomas, Roland Davide, Jack Fultz, and the legendary Johnny Kelley. Among the women, I would list Olympic gold medalist Joan Benoit, who won a gold in the first Olympic marathon for women in 1984. Others who had sensational careers and who raced in Charlie's are Lynn Jennings, Patti Catalano, Nancy Conz, Carol Cook, and Sharon Barbano. One addition I need to mention—Dick and Richard Hoyt, the father-and-son wheelchair team who have a statue at the starting line of the Boston Marathon and received an ESPY in 2012, competed in Charlie's in only their second completion back in 1977.

Lastly, in 1984 Charlie's Surplus Ten-Mile Road Race became ranked in the top one hundred road races/marathons in the world. At that point we were not just a national-class event. Little Charlie's Surplus had hit the jackpot. Congratulations were due our dad; everyone had found out what his family had known forever. Charlie Epstein was world-class. Well done Dad!

* * *

It was about this time that I found myself involved in many local nonprofit organizations around town. Even though I haven't lived in Worcester for over thirty years, the three that remain very dear to my heart are the Worcester Jewish Community Center, the Worcester Boys' Club, and an organization called To Your Health. The latter was a state-funded agency that I became the director of that promoted healthy living for students all over Massachusetts.

As this book moves forward, you will read of many of the most famous sports figures the world has ever seen, all of whom I have met, and many of whom I have been involved with. I have been in the right places at the right times because of some of my closest friends. One such friend was my best man, Brian Hammel, who never forgot me. I will say this, I did develop some nice relationships with a few of these figures, but if I were to put together a dinner for only four, I would not invite even one of those celebrities to join me. As I mention several of them in this book, I will not say anything negative about anyone. If you notice I don't compliment them, though, you can make your own judgments. Once you spend any time with any celebrity, you start to get immune to being starry-eyed. At least I have. My homeboys would get invites to the dinner, though.

Once a year before Christmas, Charlie's Surplus, my dad, and I would host a men's only sports night dinner. It was held in a large hall at an Elks Club in Worcester. It was an absolute blast. It was put on for Dad's farmer friends, business executives, local politicians, personal friends, media representatives and some of the biggest names in the world of American sports. Oh, my goodness, did we all have a blast! It was an evening that everyone talked about all year long and that many people I knew would ask if they could get an invite to.

The jokes, stories, and drinks flowed freely. We had a couple of security workers at the doors so anybody who had not been invited could not crash the party. Even to this day, almost thirty years later, I feel I'm going to burst out laughing every time I think of those special evenings.

Our master of ceremonies every year became one of the Epstein family's closest friends. Richie Hebner, the former Pittsburgh Pirates slugging third baseman, was the perfect emcee. After Richie retired from playing, he became the Red Sox hitting coach for three seasons. Richie's nickname—"Hack"—is so appropriate that everyone still calls him by it. What a tremendous baseball career he had, but I'm still convinced he missed his true calling as a stand-up comedian. Richie and his dad, Bill, also had a grave-digging business that

Richie's four brothers worked at when they were not working as firemen. What a crew!

Richie helped us get some of his friends who were also playing major league baseball. Everyone loved Richie. In fact, for many years during Richie's off seasons, he and his dad would drive into Worcester from his hometown of Norwood, Massachusetts, just outside of Boston, where he had grown up, to visit with Charlie.

The entire Epstein family was really into baseball, especially our home team, the Red Sox. We had season tickets for almost twenty-five years, seven rows directly behind the Red Sox dugout. Having Richie involved with our family was a perfect match. Years later, when Charlie Epstein passed away, Richie Hebner and his dad attended the funeral. Hack recited a poem he had written as his eulogy to my dad; it was a very touching moment.

Remember, I mentioned Charlie's favorite sport was boxing. Well, one of Dad's best friends Goodie Petronelli became the trainer and manager of Middleweight Champion of the World. Goodie owned a boxing gym in Brockton, Massachusetts, the hometown of the greatest middleweight champion who ever lived, Marvelous Marvin Hagler.

The group of stars who attended the sports night were not only baseball players. We had a lot of sports represented. Some of the most famous included the following:

- American League MVP Dennis Eckersley
- Red Sox all-star catcher Richie Gedman from Worcester (who for a couple off-seasons worked at Charlie's)
- Red Sox second baseman Marty Barrett
- Red Sox Cy Young–award winner Jim Lonborg
- Orioles Cy Young–award winner Mike Flanagan
- Red Sox American League MVP and seven-time Cy Young–winner "Rocket" Roger Clemens
- Red Sox all-star pitcher Dick Radatz
- Red Sox Manager Joe Morgan
- Red Sox President Haywood Sullivan

- Haywood Sullivan's son, catcher Marc Sullivan, also attended.
- Oakland A's pitcher, the hometown boy- "The Worcester Wonder" Paul Mitchell

Sometimes the biggest stars are the hardest to get close to.

Often sports dinners include as their guests retired professional athletes. It becomes a storytelling affair at which a bunch of old men sit around and tell stories from many years before some of the attendees were even born. Most of the athletes I mentioned were still in their primes.

NBA champions Hank Finkel and Togo Palazzi, who both won their championships with the Celtics, joined in the fun. Holy Cross Basketball Coach and EPPY's all-time favorite, George Blaney attended. Of course, we had to have one of our elite marathon runners attend. Geoff Smith, who won two Charlie's Road Races as well as two Boston Marathons, came every single year. In fact, at one of his victory ceremonies in Boston he saw me in the crowd and yelled to me to make sure he was invited back to another sports dinner.

One year the athlete who caused the most excitement was the legendary Major League Rookie of The Year and the greatest one-year sensation in MLB history, Mark "The Bird" Fidrych from the Detroit Tigers. I had gotten to know The Bird a few years earlier, during his rookie year, when I had driven to Detroit with his cousin, Bobby Fidrych, a good friend of mine from college. We spent a weekend at Mark's apartment during a Tiger homestand. I have accumulated a few stories during my lifetime, but this one will have to be told in a separate book.

The biggest celebrity of all, who had so much fun the first time he came that he came back a second time, was Marvelous Marvin Hagler. Marvin brought his middleweight championship belts with him. Everyone got a chance to put them on and have a photo taken with him and the belts. Marvin was just a tremendous guy. Marvin fit right in and had a blast. We were crushed when Marvin lost to Sugar Ray Leonard in a controversial decision. Marvin told me right after his loss to Sugar Ray that one of the reasons he was thinking of retiring from boxing was he did not want to split his purses with his ex-wife. I have never seen this reason for Marvin's retirement printed in the media.

Charlie Epstein became a well-known figure all over New England. In fact, four times he was presented with the key to the City of Worcester at different events he attended throughout his lifetime by four different mayors. The beautiful thing about Dad's success and humility was he still considered himself a "peddler".

Three

TIME TO MOVE ON

I think a lot of people around Central Massachusetts, especially Worcester, were shocked when they found out I was leaving the city. It even caught a lot of my friends and family off guard. When everyone back home thought of me, they just took for granted I was a Massachusetts guy for life.

What no one knew was that I had been having thoughts about relocating almost my entire life. Like everyone else, I never thought I would ever do it.

When I was in high school, I attended a camp for Jewish youth throughout both Carolinas. The camp was located outside of Asheville in the mountains of Hendersonville, North Carolina. My mom knew the camp director and arranged for me to attend. The camp was called Camp Blue Star. What a gorgeous campground setting it was on! Living in the South started to appeal to me.

I met a nice girl about my age at camp from the town of Kinston, North Carolina. Her name is Lynne. I can't really say she was my girlfriend because we lived so far apart. We did communicate regularly all the way through college. I sometimes wonder what would have become of us if we lived closer. To this day she has been the only Jewish girl that I guess I could call a girlfriend. Facebook is awesome! Lynne graduated from the University of North Carolina at Chapel Hill and had a long career as a lawyer in Greensboro, North Carolina.

Charlie started getting a little nervous about the major retail conglomerates that had begun to show up on the business scene. He just wasn't too sure how this was going to affect the small family businesses. He was not the only owner of a small business who was starting to notice the changing of the landscape. His friends were starting to whisper about the same thing.

Water Street in Worcester is a special place not just for the Jewish community but for the entire community. The street is steeped in tremendous history going back to before the turn of the twentieth century. The amount of business activity was something to marvel at. Through the entire twentieth century, it seemed like all of Worcester would buy their bakery products, fruits and vegetables, meats, fish, and everything else that anyone could possibly need on Water Street. It was a fun place to work.

The biggest shopping day was Sunday. After church let out, you could find all of Worcester walking around in the middle of the street doing their shopping for the coming week. During election time every single state politician in Massachusetts would set up shop all over Water Street passing out pamphlets. Water Street was not just for the Jewish community. In fact, Water Street was the last street in Worcester to have cobblestones. As a little kid, I was always fascinated by the trolley tracks that were still showing.

The only place I had ever seen that reminded me of old Water Street in Worcester was the Jewish market located in old Jerusalem.

I never got caught up with what the tradition of Water Street meant to Massachusetts. To me it was a place that my dad worked. I do know it was special to him and his contemporaries. What I remember most was running up and down Water Street from the time I could walk. As I mentioned earlier, Dad never used a cash register for his business. When I was with him at work, he would always have me race down to the end of the street to Broadway's Restaurant to get change for whatever size denomination of money a customer gave to make a purchase. What still brings out a laugh from me was how I sped up to a sprint, holding my nose every single time I passed by the fish store with its doors open. To this day I can still remember how badly the fish stank. I was just a typical kid who really didn't identify with any special historic meaning that everyone else was making such a fuss over. As much as I worshipped my dad, I just wasn't sure I wanted to spend my entire life on Water Street the way he and all the other merchants had during those years.

I remarried in the early eighties and had had a family a few years later of two daughters, Brooke, and Karli. Like any dad I was crazy about my girls. In fact, I still am. It is a giant-sized blast for me to still play with them and my three grandchildren every chance I get. I am blessed.

I felt my marriage falling apart, and in fact I did end up getting divorced. My divorce was not unlike any other for parents with young children. It was tough for everyone. The divorce tore my whole family apart. After the divorce I spent almost two years living outside of Worcester in a town called Rutland. I got to spend a great deal of time with my girls and could see they were going to grow up and be well-adjusted. One day when I picked up my girls for a daddy afternoon, Brooke mentioned that the day before she had been a flower girl at Mommy's wedding. Their new stepdad turned out to be a good guy, but I never got used to hearing him also referred to as dad. The biggest problem that I still have over my divorce is the fact that other people interfered with the beautiful relationship I have always had with my daughters. This was inexcusable and shows a complete lack of character.

With the changing business climate for mom-and-pop shops, the indifference I had toward working my entire life on Water Street, and the new situation of not wanting to play tug-of-war with my daughters, my time in Worcester was about done.

I called my parents and my attorney, Burton Berg, who is like a part of my family. Everyone agreed that getting away for a few months was a great idea. Now the tricky part. I had no idea where I was going, what I was going to do, and how long I would stay. Now, as I am writing this book, I find myself laughing. It has been well-documented that change can be tough on anyone. In fact, the three different areas of change for any adult that cause the most stress are relocation, a change of career, and a divorce. Bang! I had hit the trifecta.

I needed to devise a plan. I sat down with my entire support group, which included my parents, Burton Berg, my counselor, and a couple of close friends. Since there was only a month left before Christmas, Dad asked me to stay for the busy retail season and not leave until afterward. That was fine with me.

After the holidays I decided to stay on the East Coast and find a city of similar size to Worcester with a warm climate. I pulled out a map. My old fascination with *Black Like Me* inspired me to explore what it would be like to live in the Deep South. My top choices became Wilmington, North Carolina; Jacksonville, Florida; both Charleston and Myrtle Beach in South Carolina; Orlando and the Tampa, Florida, areas.

I thought Charleston might work out well for a few months. Remember, I had no idea how long I was going to stay or if I was ever going to make Worcester home again.

Some of this might seem a little dramatic. Well, if you put yourself in my shoes, it was. A couple of months ago someone asked me what had brought me to Charleston. As I told her a short version, she replied, "How romantic." Trust me, I have lived in Charleston, South Carolina, for almost thirty-two years, and *romantic* is the very last word I could possibly use to describe my journey down south.

My plan was to get a furnished apartment for three months in Charleston, stay until my lease expired, and return to Massachusetts when the weather turned warm in the early spring. Maybe!

My parents did not want me working in any capacity when I settled into my new digs. They thought it might be a good idea just to lie low and rest up. They both had been very generous parents to all their children, and they reassured me of financial support if I needed it. I agreed with them at the time that I would not look for work right away.

I was not just nervous; I was beyond petrified! Here I was going into a new part of the country that would be the opposite in culture and some social values of where I grew up in Worcester. I always said if I could have taken just one friend with me, it would have made me relax a little. No one—I knew no one. I did not even know how to get to Charleston. Of course, I started having lots of reservations. Who would not?

The month of December in 1988 went by amazingly fast. Business was booming at Charlie's Surplus. I was glad I was staying through the holidays to help my best buddy. I was starting to gain a little confidence about my upcoming journey. Mom and Dad were giving me pep talks at the time and reminding me that I would never be alone. A few of my best friends were reinforcing the same things to me.

The day I chose for departure, Christmas, was getting closer. Since we were Jewish, the date made a lot of sense to me and my family. The trip was going to take two days of driving. I was going to take the van I used for work at Charlie's.

I had a fantastic relationship with my girls. It was extremely important that they absolutely knew beyond any shadow of a doubt that their dad would never ever leave them. There was no question in my mind that their mom and their stepdad would be there for them. In fact, they knew whenever they wanted to call, I would drop everything and talk with them any time of day or night.

I was given a good luck party by some of my buddies a few days before I left. Did you notice I did not say farewell party? Everyone knew how much I loved my hometown and that I would never turn my back completely on Worcester.

I was at the point of no turning back. It was getting awfully close to the time I would be saying goodbye.

How do you say goodbye to all you have ever known? I loved my family and friends, my dad's friends, Charlie's Surplus, and the amazing experiences I had shared with my dad. I knew I would miss the New England basketball community; my teammates at Worcester State; the Worcester Jewish Community Center; the Red Sox, the Celtics, the Patriots; and my entire life in Worcester.

It was time to pack!

Four

GOODBYE

Christmas Eve came, and my brother Eppy drove out to my apartment in Rutland. I knew Eppy was taking my move hard. I felt bad for him. It was difficult for me to look him in the eye. We had shared the experience of being young boys who had fallen in love together with our sport of basketball. We had achieved some success with our dad in our favorite sport in Worcester's semipro summer league at Crompton Park. We shared the same friends. Eppy kept repeating over the previous two years how proud he was of me. I understood why he said that. I was not sure I could keep from falling apart if he said that to me again that night. I certainly have always been proud of all his accomplishments throughout his life. Eppy and I loved to argue about sports. Some may have thought we were not that close.

A fun memory I'll always have of Eppy is his work as a barber. Eppy had a barber shop inside of Charlie's for a few years that was called, EPPY'S Barber Shop. The only haircut that Eppy ever gave me was whan Dad held me down and Bobby carved a cross in my hair. Like they say during the NCAA Basketball Tournament, I was one and done. Over the thirty-two years I have lived in Charleston and the almost two hundred trips I have made back to my hometown there was never one time that we didn't find the time to get together for a visit. The only others that I can say that about were my daughters and parents. Eppy helped me carry the boxes to my van. I was bringing only a few boxes of clothes. I did not need that much. I had signed a lease for a furnished apartment in Charleston for three months earlier in the week. I was scheduled to move into it on December 29.

To this day I believe in all my heart, when my brother and I packed my van, he was the only person who knew I would never be returning home to live there. I wasn't even sure of that. What I decided to do was to keep my apartment in Massachusetts for four months in case I did decide to return. I thought at least I would have a place to live if that was going to be the case.

I followed Bobby to my parents' house to spend the night before I was to leave in the morning. My parents' next-door neighbor and my dear mentor from Trade, Don Lemenager, was having his annual Christmas Eve party. Once again, he called and invited my whole family to join his. I really loved going over to the Lemenagers for the holidays. In fact, as I was growing up, Don and his wife Lee would invite me over to help them decorate their tree every Christmas season.

I was hoping they would have the same entertainment at their home that they had had the previous year. Little Alisan Porter, who became a well-known singer later in life, was there to lead everyone in Christmas caroling. Young Alisan was only six, but even then, you could see her special gift. Just a couple of short years ago, Alisan won the highly popular national TV singing competition *The Voice*. Both of her parents, Laura, and Ric, remain good friends to this day.

The spirit and friendship I felt that evening was the perfect boost I needed before I was to set sail in the morning.

I woke at about 8:00 a.m. on Christmas Day. My mom made a light breakfast for me, and I knew it was time to go. Even now, as I write this book, I get emotional. I said my goodbyes to my dad and brother, and they both wished me good luck and reminded me I was only a phone call away if I ever needed anything.

The day before I left, my daughter Brooke gave me her head-band to wear for good luck, and I was wearing it around my neck that morning. That headband I did not take off for the first month in Charleston. I kept that headband hanging on my bedpost for over twenty years. In fact, I still have it hanging in my sports office at my home today in Mount Pleasant, South Carolina, over thirty years later.

Now, up to this point, people may be wondering about the relationship I had with my mom. I spend a great deal of time talking about my dad, Charlie Epstein. Sure, I spent a lot of my time with Dad. We had a blast together and accomplished some things that most fathers and sons can only dream about. Here is the thing about my mama, as I sometimes called her. I would not have accomplished anything without her. I mean nothing. I get all my fighting spirit from Sarah Epstein. Yes, Dad was tough, but not only was my mom just as tough, but she also remains one of the smartest people I have ever known. I have relied on my mom for her wisdom and encouragement in everything I have ever accomplished in my life.

From my struggles with my academics growing up and during my years at Trade to my years at WSU and my master's program in Charleston (which I will be writing about later), I would have accomplished none of it without my mom, absolutely none of it. I owe her so much for never quitting on me. When I received the master's degree from the Citadel, I placed my diploma in the mail and dedicated it to her. Mama wasn't the only one who shed a few tears the day she received it, that's for sure.

I gave my mom a big hug and kiss without looking at her for fear we might both break down. I walked out the door, got into my van, and drove away balling my eyes out. I mean balling my eyes out for two straight days all the way to Charleston. It was the longest drive of my life.

I remember almost every mile of the drive down Interstate 95 SOUTH. I had to concentrate so hard so my tears wouldn't blind me. I tried to stay focused, but it was hard. I knew what I was leaving but had no earthly idea what I was heading into. I had my road map from AAA to prevent me from getting lost.

41

I remember going through the toll booths in New York, New Jersey, and Delaware. The reason I remember the toll booths was that I could not look at the toll collectors. I didn't want them to see me crying. I was afraid they might have thought I had just murdered someone and might call the state police on me.

I made it to Richmond, Virginia, after one day of driving. I ate dinner at a Howard Johnson's and grabbed a room at the Red Roof Inn for a night. Remember, this was Christmas night, so there really wasn't too much open. I was emotionally exhausted from not only the drive but also from the past two years as well. I made a few phone calls to my family to let them know where I was staying and that I was OK. I had driven about ten hours, so I only had about seven hours left to drive the next day.

I slept in, which for me isn't that unusual, and left Richmond for the second part of the journey at 11:00 a.m. The second part of the trip was a lot easier than the day before. I had gained my composure and was now looking forward to arriving in Charleston and starting the adventure of my life.

I got to Charleston at about five-thirty in the evening. It was still light, which I was happy about because I tend to get lost easily. For dinner I ate a cheeseburger and French fries at a Waffle House. I had never eaten at a Waffle House before, and I never did again. It was disgusting!

I asked the waitress if she knew of a clean and safe motel that I could stay at for a few days before my lease started at the apartment, I had waiting for me. She mentioned that there was a Hampton Inn close by that was reasonable. It sounded rather good. When I checked in, I noticed a sign that said, "Welcome to North Charleston." I was told by the receptionist that the city of Charleston was another fifteen miles on Interstate 26. I asked the clerk many times over if the Hampton Inn was in a safe part of town. She reassured me that I had nothing to worry about and that I would be fine.

Welcome to Charleston, big boy!

Five

IN SEARCH OF MYSELF
IN CHARLESTON

The years rolled slowly past
And I found myself alone.
I found myself seeking shelter against the wind.
—BOB SEGER, "RUNNING AGAINST THE WIND"

I was emotionally and physically tired during my first couple of weeks in Charleston. I was sleeping well into the midafternoons. When I did leave the hotel, I was out exploring my new hometown.

I was trying to find different events or places that I had enjoyed back in Worcester. Much to no one's surprise, I found myself inside a college basketball field house watching a holiday high school basketball tournament my second evening in Charleston. I was already feeling a little more comfortable.

What I didn't know before I moved was that Charleston was home to three division-one university basketball programs. Now we're talking my language. I had already found all three campuses and attended home basketball games at all three universities less than two weeks into my stay. Also, I got to know all the coaches a short time later.

I moved out of my hotel on December 29, as scheduled. I found the apartment I had already signed a lease for the day before. I was in total shock. The apartment development was brand-new and gorgeous. The grounds were immaculate. There was a large swimming pool and an indoor social lounge with all the fixings, including a fireplace.

Ashley Crossings had a beautiful pond with a couple of boats that its guests could use anytime. There was also a three-mile running trail on the perimeter. I was starting to feel comfortable.

I started noticing that Southern women were not only attractive but also had a healthy glow about them. One night early on, I went out downtown to historic East Bay Street. East Bay and the adjacent Market Street were the town's hot spots. My first night down there, I was standing in a corner checking out the landscape when I found myself having my first interaction with an attractive female Charlestonian.

I was asking a lot of questions about Charleston's social landscape. She was curious to find out who I was and what I was doing in Charleston. I told her I had just gotten into town and didn't know how long I was staying. Her name was Ann. Ann asked me if I had ever heard of Kiawah Island. I told her I had not. Much to my shock, she asked me if I would like to take a ride with her out to visit the beaches on the island on New Year's Day. After a short pause of less than one tenth of a second, I said, "I'd love to."

Now, I must explain a few things. My friendship with Ann became nothing more than a platonic friendship. I was not out looking for any type of a serious relationship during my first few years in Charleston. I mean, I was petrified just thinking about one. I was in rather good shape in those days, and I was pretty fast whenever I thought anyone had different intentions than I did.

Ann picked me up at my apartment like she promised, and we had a chance to talk during the forty-five-minute drive to Kiawah. Ann told me she also had just divorced. That made me feel a lot better.

This is the time to explain something extremely important about me. I came to Charleston with zero trust in everyone I was meeting and getting to know. This became not just a Charleston feeling. This became a problem that developed and that I have lived with for over thirty years. I know a lot of people do not trust people right away. If you ask Barbara and some of my closest homeboys, they will tell you the same thing about me. I must be with someone who I have known for a long time before I will allow myself to be placed in a group social setting. This probably will take a few people by surprise. I have an extremely outgoing personality, so I'm sure people will think I'm exaggerating this point a little. Just ask my daughters; they have had to deal with it for a long time now. Just because I know lots of people and refer to them as friends my trust is with only a handful and they know who they are.

Ann and I arrived on the beach on Kiawah Island, and I just about fell over. I have never seen such a magnificent ocean view in my life. Simply breathtaking! The world-famous Ocean Course at Kiawah has played host to several major golf tournaments since it opened in 1991. For many years after that initial visit, I made Kiawah my home away from home. It seemed like every weekend I would drive to Kiawah and enjoy its beaches, running trails, and the amenities at the private pool for property owners only (*wink*).

It was at this moment I developed a hunch I might be making Charleston my home for a long time, but I wasn't 100 percent sure. I did know that my friendship with Ann had come at a great time.

On my second day in Charleston, I stopped by the Jewish Community Center in town. I was never overly religious, but I was very loyal and a believer to my heritage. Everyone was quite welcoming. They invited me to attend the New Year's Eve party they were hosting in two days. It sounded rather good because I did not want to spend New Year's Eve by myself in a new city.

The party was a blast. I was the only single person out of about one hundred married couples. I was even invited to a house party the next evening. It seemed like everything was moving in the right direction.

Let me tell you about the Charleston weather. When I moved to the Charleston Lowcountry, the area was still thought of as a hidden gem. Ten years later Charleston exploded. No longer were the northern retirees picking just Florida as their destination. Charleston had hit the map in a big way. Tourism was booming. The beaches were becoming one of Charleston's biggest attractions. The restaurants and the chefs were amazing. Soon Charleston was annually listed as the number one tourist destination city in the world by *Travel and Leisure* magazine. Charleston is big-time and deserves the ranking.

I was enjoying the outdoor winter weather to continue the sport of long-distance running. Not only was I running for exercise, but I was also running from a few members of the Jewish community who had "a nice Jewish girl I just had to meet." I'm not being cocky; I was scared to let anyone get too close.

I appreciated everyone who was looking out for me. I still do appreciate those wonderful people who went out of their way to make me feel comfortable. I just wasn't ready for anything serious. Also, I didn't want a formal date because my trust level was at below zero.

I thought maybe I was going to stay in Charleston for at least three months. I felt that was a long time to go just playing around without any type of employment. I did not think it was fair to anyone in my family to have to support me.

It was time to look for a job. I was offered several job opportunities after I was interviewed by an employment agency. I was offered work as a tool salesman, a copy machine salesman, a salesclerk at a clothing store, and a home alarm salesman.

I did not want to take a job out of desperation. If I was going to enter the workforce, I wanted it to be something I was interested in. I filled out an application with the Charleston County School District. I thought maybe I could work two or three days per week as a substitute teacher. That way I would still have time to run all over the historic section of Charleston's Battery.

Oh my, what beautiful scenery as one looks out at the Ashley River that connects to the Atlantic Ocean. I found it invigorating to run along the horses and carriages that circled the downtown area with tourists. I do not feel there is a more charming city than Charleston, with its magnificent antebellum mansions. Its amazing history is truly one of a kind. As you walk along the historic Battery, you can look out and see the world-famous Fort Sumpter, where the first shot of the Civil War was fired.

Six

First Job

I thought it might be a good time to pull out my Worcester State University diploma. The Charleston County School District has been a tremendous employer since the first day I walked into the personnel department. It was in between semesters after Christmas, so the timing couldn't have been better to be looking for a job within the school system. The personnel director offered a listing of many openings. He gave me a choice of several to select from. The opening as a career counselor for two high schools jumped right off the page.

I was excited to find a job as a substitute counselor for the entire second semester of the school year. A certification wasn't needed for the job because I was only going to have it for a few months, and the pay was on a day-by-day basis. Immediately, I knew I had found a perfect match. The two schools were quite different. James Island is a middle-class, older community with a tremendous history. People feel incredible pride about their James Island High School.

The other high school, St. John's High, is a small public high school on rural John's Island, located just outside of Charleston. The reason this is a great place in the book to give a brief description of each is because later they both became a huge part of my own Charleston history.

The principal at James Island, Floyd Hiott, was just a tremendous man. One of the finest people I have ever met. From day one we hit it off, and not only did he become my first boss, but he also became like my family. Mr. Hiott understood my situation—that I was by myself and new to the area—and he looked out for me. I loved my time working for the students at James Island for those short five months.

Simultaneously working at St. John's gave me an opportunity to work at two totally different environments. James Island is located on the outskirts of Charleston, while St. John's High is a rural community on the way to Kiawah Island. It really helped me to understand the diverse community of the Charleston Lowcountry. Both faculties rolled out the red carpet in welcoming me.

You cannot come into a new region of a country acting as if you have all the answers. Listening and asking lots of questions helped establish a good relationship with both faculties. One of my biggest strengths with young people has always been my ability to relate to their needs and interests. Especially when it's time to talk about different sports, the conversation has always been pretty easy for me to participate in.

The time as a substitute went be quickly. The experience was fantastic. There was so much that I learned during those months, and I believe it was a positive experience for the students. It was good for them to meet a person from another place who had grown up differently than one does in the South Carolina Lowcountry.

Mr. Hiott encouraged me to use my teaching degree. He strongly suggested going out to teach for a few years in North Charleston. He thought the more diverse experiences I had under my belt, the better educator I would be for the rest of my career. He made a promise that when I earned my master's degree, he would hire me back with the first counselor job vacancy that came open at James Island. What a man of his word he was.

I told you Floyd Hiott was a great friend.

Seven

BLACKS IN EDUCATION

Charleston was suddenly feeling more like home, but I was still thinking of moving on to Florida. The turning point was when Mr. Floyd Hiott brought me down to the Citadel Military College of South Carolina and introduced me to Dr. Ken Shelton, the dean of the graduate school's education department.

Both Mr. Hiott and Dr. Shelton thought I had a great future as a high school counselor and encouraged me to enroll in the master's program for counselor education. It was a tremendous idea.

I am sure no one back home in Worcester could have imagined a master's degree program was going to be part of my three-month journey to Charleston.

The first course that I was enrolled in started that June. The course was career counseling, which was taught by my advisor, Dr. Shelton. It was during the first class that Dr. Shelton explained the big project of the term. He asked the students to select a nontraditional career and interview ten people who are employed in that field. "Blacks in Education" sounded like it would be fun to explore. I turned in my choice of project during the second class. It was then that Dr. Shelton asked me to meet him in his office. I was quite nervous because I didn't know what he wanted to see me for.

Dr. Shelton reminded me in our meeting that I was now living in the South and I should move slowly as I worked on my project. At first, I thought I was being intimidated. The Citadel had a bad history with its undergraduate college; racial and gender discrimination are part of its dark past.

After several more classes, I could see that Dr. Shelton was going to be someone whom I could trust and that he was only giving me some advice based on his own knowledge and experiences.

I worked throughout the course on my project, and I was getting lots of positive feedback not only from my professor but from all ten black educators I was interviewing. Well-thought-out questions were asked, and the stories that were being shared were extraordinary. Stories from the segregated South became a common theme. The interviews were all being tape-recorded, and they were later turned in with the written report.

What an educational experience it was. The educators expressed the personal obstacles they had endured going through South Carolina's public education system during the fifties through the seventies. The lack of operation funds given to the segregated schools—compared to white peer institutions—was alarming to hear about.

Some talked about their experiences of being the first students to integrate into schools that became part of the civil rights movement. I learned more about my new home than I ever could have imagined.

I remember that the ten educators never showed any anger in their voices while they talked of their experiences. They lived during a terrible time, but they seemed to be thankful that the country's education system had come a long way. A few of the people interviewed talked about how important it was that they had sacrificed for the betterment of their children and their grandchildren. A recurring theme was how far the education system in Charleston had come but how far it still had to go.

Much to my surprise, I received A's both on my project and in the course. Later that summer Dr. Shelton pulled me aside and told me he was proud of the work that was turned in on my project, "Blacks in Education." He also said that I had selected a difficult topic to research and that it was professionally handled. His words were very reassuring—my coursework was off to a good start, and there was mutual respect between the dean of education at the Citadel Graduate College and his new student.

Eight

WHERE IS THE BERRY?
1989–1990

As much as I wanted to earn a bachelor's degree from WSU, I wasn't sure I was ever going to use it. Well, it sure did come in handy in South Carolina. What a great lesson I had been taught. You just never know in life where you will end up and what you'll be doing. Nothing can be more valuable than your education, no matter where your journey may take you. If you don't think I didn't share this lesson a few hundred times over, think again. Thank goodness for WSU!

My teaching certification is in elementary education. It was time to interview at several elementary schools and hope for the best.

Where is Berry Elementary School? I drove around North Charleston for close to an hour before my interview there. Earlier I mentioned that I tend to get lost frequently. After a brief conversation with the principal, I was given a tour of the school campus. The principal had a wonderful personality. What I didn't know before I arrived is that Berry had only one male working at the school. That male was the day porter. The principal also mentioned how she loved my loud, deep voice. It was the first time I had ever heard that.

There was absolutely no doubt in the principal's mind that she wanted me as her fifth-grade language arts teacher. She wasn't the least bit concerned that I had never taught before. There was lots of concern in my mind about that small detail, though. She promised me the kids would just love me and that the boys would enjoy learning about basketball in addition to language arts. I wasn't totally convinced, however, that Berry was a good fit for me.

It was important to me that my first teaching job would be a good match. I wanted more time to interview with other schools. That night the principal called me and made another pitch. Finally, she had her male teacher for fifth-grade language arts.

One month later there was an orientation for all the teachers at Berry a few days before the school year was to begin. As all the faculty were introducing themselves, something important jumped out. There were thirteen teachers in the entire school, and seven, including me, were first-year teachers from out of state.

Three especially important points I'm going to make here. Number one, if you're a first-year teacher, make absolute sure you're at a school that will offer you a faculty that has more than a couple of experienced teachers to help you get through that first year. It is imperative that you have a mentor assigned to you, so you have a go-to advocate and support system available whenever you need one. Trust me, eventually you will need one. Number two, if you are new to an area, always drive around the neighborhood before you sign a contract so that you know where the students you will be teaching, are growing up. Thirdly, if you're starting at a school where more than half of the faculty are first-year teachers from out of state, that is clearly a red flag that you better be prepared to deal with.

The third point still infuriates me. Schools, as we know, are not built for the adults. "*Students first*" is what most educators clearly understand. It is totally unacceptable to have most of a faculty come from out of state into a neighborhood school where the students are crying out for mentors and role models. Of course, students can develop strong relationships with new and out-of-state teachers. The point is, why put our students in that position? Students need role models that they can relate to. Why make students wait almost half the year before they decide if they can trust the adults that have been given the tough task of educating them?

A principal should stress as part of the interview process the demographics of the feeder neighborhoods. The lack of diversity in a school needs to be understood before the students arrive. The proportion of first-year teachers we had at Berry indicated, even before the first day of class, that the new staff members were going to face several challenges.

The feeder neighborhood for Berry was a large development that consisted of old dwellings. Many of these homes were run-down and unkept. The neighborhood was located behind Berry. It is called Liberty Hill. It had a reputation as a socioeconomically depressed inner-city community, with lots of drugs that had become a serious problem for everyone living there. Liberty Hill is unique. It is built in an exceptionally large circular rotary that consists of a couple hundred small houses.

In the last decade, the city of North Charleston has worked with a couple of developers, and anyone who has not seen Liberty Hill for many years would never be able to recognize the neighborhood, except for the location. What is even better, the new homes are federally funded based on income. It is thrilling to see North Charleston helping to restore a better quality of life for its residents without displacing them and adding to the problem of gentrification that other cities in America are dealing with.

Mr. Hiott gave me the best advice I ever received in education. Teachers should not take a job at a school and remain there until they retire. Teaching should not be about finding a comfort zone. The best way for educators to grow professionally is to have diverse teaching experiences throughout a full career. I have seen this occur many times in my career. So many educators enjoy working close to their homes, and they do not want to budge. A lot of them are terrific teachers. But they have never experienced anything except teaching children who are growing up in their neighborhoods. They develop no point of reference.

This is not just about the better high schools I have worked at. This situation also occurs in communities whose schools are Title I schools or less high-achieving ones. It is so easy for any professional in any occupation to become stagnant.

In education it isn't just about teaching the core curriculum; a lot of times that is the easy part. Most teachers learn this after a fairly short time. Students come to school with many social problems that some teachers must deal with daily. If a teacher has never had to teach students who are homeless, hungry, cold, dirty, or dealing with other challenging socioeconomic situations, then they are working in a perfect world. I know the America I'm living in today is far from a perfect world. Perfect worlds can be counterproductive when it comes to growing personally and professionally.

During my first week at Berry, my principal met with me and shared the South Carolina standard test scores for the fifth graders from the previous year. I knew this was going to be a challenging year.

One percentile was the score I was being asked to improve on. That's right, my fifth graders were being asked to improve on the lowest language arts scores in the state of South Carolina. I was never big on using grades or test scores as the primary or only indicator for student achievement. But let us face it, one percentile is downright heartbreaking.

The principal had mentioned Berry's goals for test scores for the year to my students. I decided I was not going to constantly remind my students every day how poorly the school had done the previous year. It was mentioned once, and after that I left it alone. I did not want that burden on my students or myself.

I placed a big banner across the front of the classroom, and every morning, after I took attendance, we all recited the words on the banner: "Challenge Yourself Toward Greatness" became our class moto for the year.

We worked hard that year. My students did everything in their power to close the achievement gap. They read and wrote stories every single day. Phonics were taught and reinforced again and again.

Fighting became a common occurrence, unfortunately. Seeing as I was the only male teacher in the school, I found myself being the disciplinarian for several teachers on my hall. During parent conferences I did notice how young some of the parents were. Some were no more than in their middle to late twenties.

The funniest thing that happened that year took place on the first day of the school year. Like I mentioned earlier, I was in rather good shape back in the late eighties from my own conditioning. I thought I would bring my running shoes to work with me and during recess I would challenge the students to a race. It was a tremendous idea, except for one small detail—my students were more than ready for the challenge.

The first day of school was in late August that year. The temperature was in the mid-nineties when the races began. I won the first race against the entire student body, not just my classroom of students. By now I think you can all guess what happened. Yup, I was dripping in sweat and exhausted, and the kids were going absolutely nuts over their new crazy teacher. We raced three or four more times and I finished last each time. When recess ended the kids were so fired up, we couldn't get them in. For the rest of the afternoon all I heard was, "Are we going to do this every day?" School could not have ended quick enough that first day; I needed to get home, shower, and take a long nap. That was a short-lived idea. What had I been thinking?

I wish I could say the year went by quickly. My first year of teaching at Berry Elementary School in North Charleston, South Carolina, was a long year for all of us.

Testing week came in April, and I would have bet any amount of money my students were going to get their test scores up to at least the eighteenth-to-twentieth-percentile level of all fifth graders in South Carolina. They had worked hard and stayed motivated for the challenge all year.

The first visitor we had in our class that year besides the principal was the test coordinator for the entire Charleston County School District. The first day of testing, the coordinator stayed for the entire three hours of testing without any advanced notice. The fifth-grade language arts class at Berry Elementary School in North Charleston was on the South Carolina Department of Education's radar. Make no mistake about that.

Yes, the students improved, and I was immensely proud of how they had matured throughout the year, but my expectations were way off. I am glad I never mentioned the goals I had for the class before testing, or I think they would have been deflated. It was disappointing that the students were only able to raise their test scores to the five-percentile level. When the scores were announced to them, they were all proud they were no longer at the very bottom of South Carolina. I was happy for them also. It must have been a heavy burden they were carrying that year. We had a party at the end of the school year so they could have a nice memory to carry with them to middle school. This is the very first time I have ever mentioned to anyone that I was a little disappointed. The disappointment did not last long, though.

New contracts came out, and I decided to turn mine back in without signing it. One year was enough. Of course, I still think about my students from that year. How can I ever forget April, Nicole, Bertha, Jeremy, Marquis, Terrance, Keith, and all the others? A few I'm friends with on Facebook. Others, I still worry about to this day. All teachers are like that.

At an annual salary of eighteen thousand dollars, it was the hardest I had ever worked. It is a good thing I had some financial help from my parents, or I would have never been able to make my child support payments.

To this day I consider my one year at Berry Elementary the most valuable year of my life. My kids made a man out of me that year.

I finally had experienced what I had read about back in fifth grade. Segregation was still alive and well in South Carolina in 1989.

I have told many college students studying to be educators the following: "Have a couple of diverse experiences in your career. If you aren't comfortable after a year or two, find a more suitable situation." This advice, which I was given by Mr. Hiott, might be the most valuable lesson that I was given during my career in Charleston. This is the reason that after I left Berry, I had four of the most diverse experiences in the Charleston County School District that any educator could have experienced. The hardest part of these changes became the most rewarding; being forced out of one's comfort zone creates a higher level of self-learning, and isn't that what education should be about for everyone?

It was time to move into a small home in a section of Charleston called Shadowmoss Plantation. The two-bedroom home had just been rebuilt after it had been destroyed by Hurricane Hugo in September of 1989. The home was on the golf course in Shadowmoss. It was nice to live in a neighborhood setting again. I love watching the kids riding their bikes all over the place. It was reminiscent of the neighborhood in Worcester I was living in before my divorce. I would stay in this house in Shadowmoss for six years, until I married Barbara Lindsay.

Worcester Mayor Tim Cooney sitting on the Charlie Epstein
Monument at ELM PARK Worcester, Mass

Mark "Pathfinder" showing off his gold medal with the entire USA
Maccabi Men's Basketball Team in Sydney Australia 2006

Students at James Island High getting ready to run with the Olympic Torch during the SC Prom Promise Campaign of 1996.

Pathfinder and Baseball great Ozzie Smith, Look at the trade Pathfinder just made, Ozzie is now donning a RED SOX cap.

Mark entering the dungeon at the Cape Coast Slave Castle Africa.

Classroom of kindergarten students at a primary school in Accra, Ghana

ENTIRE CAMP PHOTO AT THE BILL RUSSELL ADULT FANTASY CAMP
LOS VEGAS. Take a look at the front row, Not a bad all-star team!

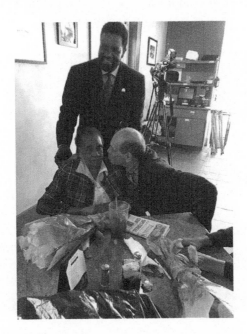

Pathfinder giving a kiss to Coretta Scott's cousin- Christine
Jackson as Representative Wendell Gilliard looks on.

Diane Epstein addressing the crowd at Charlie Epstein
Day in 2019 at ELM PARK Worcester.

Mark "Pathfinder" fighting every tooth and nail to change
the public school dropout age in SC from 17 to 18.

My two best buddies Jim Burke and Brian Hammel who both could play some hoop in their day showing off a few of their championship basketball trophies that they won for Charlie's Surplus.

This is the Dad's favorite, summer fun with his little angels, Brookie and Karli Alexis.

Charlie Epstein 'The Peddler" showing off his first car, late 1940's.

One of my favorite all-time athletes. Eric Dickerson is just a lot of
fun to hang with. Tremendous player, but a much better guy.

God Bless "Beautiful Barbara", another anniversary. I owe my love BIG TIME!

Pathfinder with baseball MVP's Dennis Eckersley and Roger
Clemens at a Charlie's Holiday Sports Party-1986

"Boston" Billy Rodgers winning the inaugural Charlie's Surplus 10 Mile Road Race with Charlie clapping at Elm Park, Worcester MA, in 1976.

DAD AND MOM BEFORE CHARLIE'S ROAD RACE IN 1982.

New England Basketball Legends; Fanny Laffin, Michael Adams, and Owen Mahorn reunite with Pathfinder at the New England Basketball Hall Of Fame Induction in Worcester MA 2013.

Representative Wendell Gilliard presents Mark with his greatest honor, the MLK PICTURE AWARD FOR THE LOWCOUNTRY OF SC in 2016.

DAD!

THE GREAT, JULIUS "DR J" ERVING.

Pathfinder with Barry Bonds and David "The Admiral" Robinson at the PUMP FOUNDATION GALA Beverly Hills Hilton Las Angeles 2013.

My ONLY SPORTS HERO, THE GREATEST,

Coach BILL RUSSELL!

Goodwill Students at West Ashley High

RED SOX STARS Marty Barrett and Dick Radatz along with Great Britain, Olympic and Marathon Great Geoff Smith hanging with MiddleWeight Champion Marvelous Marvin Hagler at Charlie's Holiday Party in 1987.

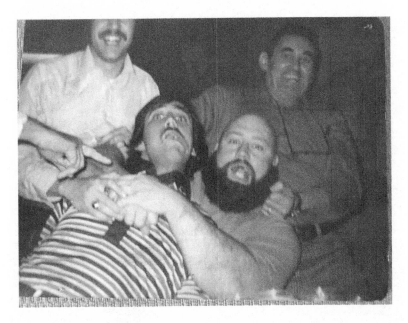

Bugsy McGraw puts Pathfinder in a choke hold in 1976 as
DAD cheers for the body slam at the PNI, Worcester

Epstein family friend, baseball legend Richie Hebner with Charlie and
a young Pathfinder in 1980 at Charlie's Annual Sport's Night.

The Pride Of Worcester, RED SOX All-Star catcher Richie Gedman
and Bobby Epstein enjoying Charlie's big bash in 1983.

Proud First grade teacher with her daughter in Africa

Nine

NORTH CHARLESTON HIGH SCHOOL, 1990–1993

I left Berry Elementary with the experience level of a twenty-year teacher.

The interview process is a big game that I was dreading to have to go through again. I sent out my résumé to seven principals, all of whom were in the Charleston County School District. A few weeks went by, and I hadn't heard back from anyone yet.

Coaching basketball was on my radar. While at Berry I was driving to James Island High every day after school and working as the assistant basketball coach for the boys' varsity at James Island. I was hoping to combine both jobs at my next stop.

One night I got a call from the new principal at North Charleston High School (NCHS). Tom Mullins had just been hired. He wanted to meet with me the next day. When we met, I was a little surprised to find out Mr. Mullins knew a few things about me already. North Charleston was not on my radar yet. It was a fun interview because Tom wanted to talk my language. He wanted to talk about basketball. We hit it off, and right on the spot he offered me a teacher and basketball coaching position.

What I learned about Mr. Mullins was earlier in his career he had taught and coached basketball at North Charleston. He had been an assistant principal at Middleton High (the alma mater of Darius Rucker) in Charleston and had been given his new position just a couple of days before he called me. He mentioned that he had attended James Island's two games against Middleton the year before and had observed me coaching. He also told me that the superintendent mentioned my name to him and told him that my loud voice in the classroom gave me a good presence in front of the students.

Here is the funny thing about the strong voice that people in Charleston seemed to like. My sister, Diane, was not only concerned about my speech, which had been late in developing, but she was also convinced I talked loudly because I was hard of hearing. She wanted my mom to get me checked out with two doctors. It is such a shame that not everyone can grow up with an older sister.

The offer at NCHS couldn't have come at a better time. After signing the contract, I was able to enjoy my summer with my daughters and out at Kiawah Island.

My teaching position at NCHS was a little unique. I mentioned earlier that I was certified in elementary education. North Charleston had a program called "High School Eight." This class was made up of twenty-five students who were all overaged and in eighth grade at a middle school.

To alleviate a situation in middle school where you had eleven-year-olds attending the same middle school as fifteen- and sixteen-year-olds, they created a High School Eight class. The concept made a lot of sense. Give the overaged students in middle school a social promotion and let them go to a high school with students their own age. Hopefully, this will help give them the motivational push they need to catch up.

My job was going to be to teach the eighth-grade curriculum that they would have been taught in their home middle school. The students would not be given a promotion into ninth grade. They would be given the opportunity to take their eighth-grade curriculum at the high school with a teacher certified at the eighth-grade level. An extra bonus for them would be that twice every day they would be enrolled with the general population, taking two high school elective courses—chosen from art, music, physical education, career education, and ROTC—for high school credits. It was a great deal for the students.

I thought I was being hired as the head varsity coach. It turned out that a wonderful gentleman named Teddy Wright had been appointed the head coach, and I would work as the assistant and JV coach. Over the course of my life in basketball, I have always thought it important for the head coach to select his own assistant. It helps with communication and trust, so everyone is on the same page. With Teddy and I, there was never a problem. We ended up with a nice relationship. When he died a few years back, I lost a trusting man, and the players not only lost their coach but also a great role model.

There is another rather humorous story I'm going to share. This story is not just funny; it's still beyond my wildest imagination. Who would have ever thought when I left Worcester just eighteen months earlier, I'd be teaching language arts, earth science, and South Carolina history at North Charleston, South Carolina, in 1990? What a combination this was going to be. Even as I write this book, I must pause, shake my head, and ask myself how I got into this situation. *Earth science and South Carolina history?* Are you kidding me? I cannot tell you how many times at dinner over the past twenty-seven years I have brought it up with my wife Barbara, and we both have laughed uncontrollably. Absolutely unreal!

I remember the first day of school my first year. I was hoping that my students wouldn't take any notes from my lectures. I had no idea what I was talking about. The most difficult part of my job during those three years at NCHS was studying the student textbooks the night before each lecture, so at least I could fake it a little bit. Sometimes my lectures were so convoluted to even me that I would take a break in the middle of them and start talking about the Boston Red Sox. I hope the readers of this book don't think I'm making any of this up. It would be impossible to do so.

I was absolutely thrilled I had landed at NCHS. My classes were hysterical. I had so much fun with my students. They all found out quickly that if they wanted to get me sidetracked from teaching, all they had to do was ask me how Brooke and Karli were doing. Some of the imitations of me they would do would have me falling out of my chair. If kids know you care about them, they'll appreciate it and return the favor. What a blast I could have with some.

I always worried about teacher evaluations. I taught language arts very well, but I was petrified that if one of the assistant principals came into the class to give me a formal evaluation during a South Carolina history or earth science lecture, I would be totally screwed.

I enjoyed learning about South Carolina history. I figured it was a good opportunity to learn about the history of my new home state. By my second year, I got comfortable teaching the course. In fact, I must bring up the book *Black Like Me* again. Believe it or not, I brought the original book that I had read in fifth grade with me from Worcester and would encourage all my High School Eight students to borrow it. They thought it was cool they were reading the original book that I had read.

Let's get back to earth science again. I would confuse myself so much during my lectures that I would give everyone a test score of one hundred just for returning their tests with their name on it. Everyone would also get an A on their report cards in earth science. No wonder the students liked me. We had a giant blast together.

I hate perceptions that are made about young people. If anyone reading this book thinks that Black children don't enjoy writing, I wish you could have attended one of my language arts classes. Once a week the students would receive a topic that they would have to create a story about. It wasn't very long—about three to four hundred words. Each student would write a rough draft and edit it. Then they would rewrite the story in cursive and turn in their finished product at the end of each week. I would also write on the same topic and join in on the students' assignment. The point is if the students know that they aren't being given writing assignments as busy work or a punishment, they get to enjoy it. They also liked the fact that their teacher was joining in on their work.

As this book continues, moving through all the high schools I have worked at, I am going to continue to attack what I believe are false perceptions.

I will never forget the time Mr. Mullins approached me one day in front of my classroom door before school. He wanted to know why not one of my students had missed one day of school in two months. I told him we were having so much fun they didn't want to miss out on anything. Remember, these were all students who had fallen behind in middle school for one reason or another.

The chapter in the earth science book that screwed me up the most was the one on longitude and latitude. Oh my, oh my! No matter how long I had studied it the night before and had, shockingly, understood it, once I started teaching it, I would get myself turned upside down. I could not even follow my own thoughts. I would go home that night, reread the material, and try it the next day. Yup, I started out OK, but three minutes in, here we go again. I would have lines on the chalkboard zigzagging all over the place. Those poor kids!

South Carolina history was more enjoyable. Charleston has more history than just about any city in America. So much has been written about it over the years. As I mentioned earlier, over the last few years, Charleston has become the number one destination city in the world. People marvel at the historic district located downtown. Horses and carriages are constantly taking tourists in a big circle to show off Charleston's beautiful homes, gardens, iron gates, and landmarks. When they get off, people are enchanted by the beauty they have just witnessed and heard stories about. Of course, the visitors think they have just seen Charleston in all its splendor.

What people don't know and see is there is a lot more to Charleston, aspects of the city that the horses are not trained to show them. This is where my warped Northern humor kicked in. I used to refer to the horses and carriages being used as donkeys and buggies.

I would get my students all laughing when I would say, "Until you see the donkeys and buggies go past your home, the visitors haven't seen all that Charleston has to offer." The students would howl. You must be able to speak their language a little.

Coaching basketball went as I had expected. Coach Teddy Wright had a laid-back approach toward coaching basketball. I can be a little tough, and I emphasize playing physical and in-your-face defense. We complemented each other beautifully. We had some great teams at NCHS and some great players. They were a lot of fun to be around. Many are friends with their old coach on Facebook. I'm still enjoying their camaraderie.

The biggest disappointment I have looking back at teaching the High School Eight class is that the entire program has been done away with, districtwide, due to budget cuts. What the administrators were doing was tracking each student closely all the way to their senior years and graduation. The district didn't feel that enough students were earning their diplomas out of the program to finance it. Five to ten students from each class would end up graduating each year out of the twenty-five that had started in the program four to five years earlier. If you think about it, that means fifteen to twenty of the students from my three-year tenure ended up graduating. I thought it was worth keeping if they found the right teachers. My students did not need a taskmaster; they needed someone who would start each day letting them have a chance to talk about what was on their minds. They brought a lot of personal issues with them, and you had to let them feel special. It was during my years at NCHS that I started to pay attention to dropout rates.

My years at NCHS were priceless. I saw lots of personal hardships among the students. Their spirits, though, were unbreakable. Many in the faculty remain friends until this day.

My final word about NCHS is that, yes, you would find that many of the more than one thousand students had come from challenging socioeconomic backgrounds. Yes, most of the students were African American. Yes, several struggled with their academics. Yes, the faculty all got along well. No, we had few discipline problems.

Things have changed quite a bit in the last several years at NCHS. It breaks my heart when I hear about the few hundred students that go there now. Discipline has become a major problem, and very few white students remain. The school now is a Title I school due to the socioeconomic demographics. Changing of the times has been tough for the school.

From 1990 through 1993, there was nowhere in Charleston or the state of South Carolina I would rather have been than at North Charleston High School. Public perceptions are tough to change.

I finished work on my master's degree at the end of my third year at NCHS. Mr. Mullins approached me about the possibility of staying if a position in the NCHS Guidance Department opened. I wasn't ready to sign a contract until I explored all of the possible opportunities that might become available as the summer moved along.

I had my eyes glued to the list of district vacancies that were being published. There was no doubt in my mind where I wanted to be. I had my heart hoping that I would again become a James Island High School Trojan.

Ten

THE CITADEL GRADUATE COLLEGE, 1989–1993

Working toward a master's degree is a huge commitment. The time and work involved is enormous. I had to make sure that this effort was going to lead to what I needed in my life to continue in my new career. Once you begin investing your time, effort, and money, it is totally senseless to change your mind and discontinue moving forward.

There were many things going on in my life, just as there are for most people. The biggest question I still had was how badly I really wanted to continue to live in Charleston. Yes, I loved it in the Lowcountry.

The Lowcountry does have a couple of drawbacks for someone who grew up in the Northeast around professional sports. Driving forty miles into Boston from Worcester to watch the pro sports was something I had done thirty to forty times a year without giving it much thought.

Spending my Friday nights at the Boston Garden watching the great Celtics dynasties was a big part of my upbringing. I am not boasting in this book about anything; that's just how my closest friends and I grew up. I had Celtics season tickets for almost twenty years. We didn't realize during all those years just how lucky we were. Our human nature side made us start taking these opportunities for granted. The Atlanta and Orlando-Tampa areas were still very enticing.

Then there were my daughters. I was flying back to Massachusetts at every opportunity to make sure they would not grow up as young girls without their dad's love.

I could not stop teaching and going to graduate school. My job was important to me. Also, I had made a commitment to use my basketball background to help me get my teaching positions. So, I knew a lot of my extra time was being taken up already. All those things I mentioned made working toward a master's degree a difficult decision.

After much conversation with my mom, we both decided going back to school was worth the rewards. Mom was right again.

As I mentioned earlier, Dr. Shelton became my advisor and my professor at the Citadel in the counselor education program. The Citadel is in downtown Charleston, and this made it very convenient to take classes there. It is a good thing I enjoy learning and writing because I sure had a lot of both going on there. One thing I had totally forgotten about since I graduated from Worcester State was the camaraderie that takes place with your classmates. I really enjoyed that. I might be guarded about developing close friendships, but I do enjoy the banter that goes on outside of class about the coursework and professors.

Once again, I was given one of those provisional acceptances into the program. To receive a full acceptance, I needed to receive two As and two Bs in my first four classes. Fortunately, that's exactly what I made. I am not going to talk about my grades again, other than those I received to get a full acceptance.

It was tough enough teaching full-time, coaching basketball, and trying to be a dad from a distance. I was never a great student and had been out of college for fifteen years before I decided to get my master's. I gave away my TV and kept the curtains drawn in my home so I could minimize as many distractions as I could control. There is one small detail I have yet to mention in this book. I never learned how to type very well, (I'm shocked I'm typing this book). So, every report and project I turned in at the Citadel was typed by an extremely sweet lady named Mary Perry who lived in downtown Charleston. Ms. Perry was paid for the wonderful work she was doing and earned every penny she received.

I spent four straight summers taking classes. Also, I was taking courses during the school year while I was teaching and coaching. Talk about overload. I missed spending my entire summers with Brooke and Karli. I would always get back for at least a few weeks, though.

The Citadel has an interesting history, to say the very least. It is known as the Military College of South Carolina. There are no military obligations for undergraduates who graduate with a bachelor's degree. Wow do the students have it rough. There is no way I could have ever attended the undergraduate program. There have been many abuses carried out over the years by older cadets on their freshmen counterparts. Racism and prejudice were rampant until recently. The outrage of the public over the past few years has pressured the officers at the Citadel to tone down (hopefully) their ignorance of abuses.

Graduate students and undergrads have little contact with each other. They use the same facilities, such as classrooms, at different times. Interactions only occur if members of both groups are using the library at the same time.

It took me four exceptionally long years of taking classes part-time before I finally reached a goal that I had never dreamed was attainable. For four years, before every single test in every single course, I would call my mom to hear her voice and her words of motherly encouragement. Now you understand more fully the relationship I had with my mom, Sarah Epstein.

The first trip to Charleston for Brooke and Karli came for my graduation from the Citadel. I purposely chose this occasion to show my girls that their dad had not just been running around Charleston over the last four years. Also, I wanted to teach them a lesson about education. The lesson being that you were never too old to go back to school.

I am not going to share what my GPA was, but I remain enormously proud of it. I had finally become a great student. To this day I dedicate the master's degree from the Citadel to my mom and my two daughters.

Eleven

FRIENDSHIPS

In September of 1989, Charleston got hit with one of the worst hurricanes in US history. The devastation was incredible. The entire Lowcountry came to a complete standstill for several months. Hurricane Hugo was a big reason I wanted to move to Florida. In fact, I did travel down to Florida eight times during my first two years in Charleston to check it out. I don't think I was alone in my thinking during this time. It was during this time of recovery that I developed a special friendship with one of the nicest and kindest families I have ever met.

Dr. Richard Ulmer and his wife, Martha, became my surrogate family in Charleston. The introduction came via a chance encounter before the Furman versus Citadel football game. Before the game started, I bought a ticket from Dr. Ulmer and his wife and sat with them. Both Richard and Martha are graduates of Furman University. We started a conversation during the game based on our love for sports. After the game ended, Dr. Ulmer invited me to his family home on Farmfield Avenue in Charleston for an oyster roast party. When I arrived at the party, Ms. Martha opened the door and wasn't going to let me in. To this day we still laugh about that. I had looked a bit unkept at the game. After the game was over, I went home and cleaned up. Martha did not recognize me until I started talking in my Boston accent.

Dr. Ulmer immediately became my doctor. The Ulmer family to this day has played a huge part of my life in Charleston. Martha Ulmer calls me her "little brother." I am not sure I would have stayed in Charleston without that chance meeting. We have celebrated holidays, weddings, graduations, retirements, and so many other occasions together over the years. They also attended my daughter Brooke's wedding in Boston a few years back. It's been just wonderful to have such a phenomenal support family while living in Charleston. To this very day I visit on occasion with the family at their home in the West Ashley section of Charleston. The entire Ulmer family has truly been an important blessing in my life.

Charleston is known for its hospitality, and there are several others who have been there for me during my life in Charleston. Besides Floyd Hiott and Dr. Shelton, two especially important friends who were there for me whenever I reached out were the late Ken Burger and Gene Sapakoff.

Ken Burger died a few years ago, but his legacy and his friendship will never fade from my memory. Ken was the finest sports columnist I have ever read. He loved his life in Charleston so much he never moved away. He was so outstanding in his work I am sure he probably passed up jobs in bigger markets to remain close to his beloved Lowountry. He didn't have to take time out of his schedule during my first several years in Charleston, but he wanted to make sure I understood the nuances of my new hometown, and he did not want me to make mistakes that could cause me embarrassment or problems.

Ken's biggest legacy is to the Medical University of South Carolina (MUSC). During his last few years, Mr. Burger raised many hundreds of thousands of dollars toward prostate cancer treatment. There now stands a room at MUSC with Ken Burger's name on it, recognizing his hard work as one of Charleston's very favorite humanitarians.

Gene Sapakoff is also a sports columnist extraordinaire at the Charleston *Post and Courier*. Charleston is home to many of the most talented professionals in the world. Many could leave this incredible Lowcountry we call home for much more fame and fortune.

My friendship with Gene has been extremely important to me. I trust him. He understands how I'm wired (I think) better than everyone I know in South Carolina, other than my wife Barbara. He also has a great level of insight. When I have an idea, I usually bounce it off Gene to see what he thinks. A quick text or call to Gene, and I have the information I need to make an educated decision. What a great resource Mr. Sapakoff remains.

I do miss the Boston pro sports scene, but not as much as when I first arrived. Part of the reason is that Charleston is a major hub for minor league sports. The Yankees have a minor league affiliate in town called the Riverdogs. The organization is owned by famous actor Bill Murray.

The real reason I don't miss the games in Boston as much as I thought I would is my friend Bill Lynds and his wife, Linda, from Atlanta. My wife Barbara and I have attended over fifty Braves games with Bill and Linda in Atlanta since I moved to Charleston. I met Bill by chance at a Braves game in 1991. Bill has season tickets, and after I sat next to him for one game, we hit it off. For the last twenty-eight years, Barbara and I have been his guests in Atlanta during the summer, and we all attend a couple of games together. It was terrific to watch all those great Braves teams of the nineties. Bill and Linda redefine generosity.

Barbara and I still get back to Fenway Park in Boston for at least two to three games every year. I also go to Patriots games every year to watch Tom Brady help lead the Pats to another Super Bowl championship and to NBA games in Charlotte, Atlanta, Orlando, New York, and Boston. I definitely get my pro sports fix.

A couple of families in Shadowmoss remain friends. Both were next-door neighbors. Jerry and Debby Baker, along with Joe and Peter Bowler, could not have been nicer to me over the years. Jerry was the longtime Athletic Director at The College of Charleston. Also, Johnny Dodds and his wife, Debbie, I consider to be two people I can turn to if I ever get into a bind.

Tom Conrad was in town coaching basketball at Charleston Southern University. I had known Tom from my New England basketball days when he was coaching at St Michaels College in Vermont. Tom moved out of Charleston a few years ago when he was given the job as a scout for the Washington Wizards of the NBA. We have remained good buddies throughout the years.

Ms. Mary Runyon will always be extremely special to me. I cannot omit her name here. She was my supervisor and my leader for everything we accomplished together as a team during my ten years at West Ashley High School. I will be getting back to our work together later.

I know I refer to a lot of people I know as friends and a lot are. I just wish I could allow my seself to trust them more. I think that happens often when someone gets burned badly.

Twelve

PLAYING THE SINGLE LIFE IN CHARLESTON

Look, I'm not going to continue writing this book and pretend I've been an angel throughout my years in South Carolina. When I made my decision to go forward with this project, I knew I was going to have to be transparent and totally honest.

When I first arrived, I was struggling and not looking for any type of lasting relationships with anyone. As a few months went by and I came to feel more at home, I realized Charleston had a sensational social life for single adults.

The first young lady I dated a few times lived in my apartment complex. Her name was Katherine. One day Katherine told me her ancestors probably would not have been happy with her dating some-one from Boston. I asked her why she would say that. She later explained to me that she was related to the Late Jefferson Davis, the President of the Confederacy. I nearly fell over. Also, her great-uncle Richard Manning Jeffries had been governor of South Carolina in the 1940s. Her mom's maiden name is Manning. Sure enough, she showed me her family tree, and there it was. I'm guessing Jefferson Davis wasn't a big Red Sox fan either; that's OK, though, as long as he didn't like the Yankees.

Long-distance running became one of the first activities I participated in right after I arrived. The Lowcountry is a haven for some of
the best long-distance runners in the world. Since everything is flat
in the Lowcountry, running and racing are easy on your body. Mount
Pleasant and Charleston are both home to one of the biggest and
most popular 10K races in the world. Over forty thousand runners
and walkers line up the first Saturday of every April and celebrate a
community event like no other I have ever witnessed. The race starts
in Mount Pleasant and goes over the Ravenel Bridge and ends up at
Marian Square in downtown Charleston.

The Cooper River Bridge Run serves as the kingpin for many
other smaller races held in South Carolina throughout the year. That
is why I'm bringing it up. It helps motivate many to get out and exercise and enjoy a healthier lifestyle.

I started looking at the race calendar immediately and joining
in the local weekend races. I was not only running against stiff competition, but I was also getting my exercise and meeting people who
shared a healthy, common interest.

When I first arrived in town, I heard a lot of people talking about
this annual arts and music festival that comes around in May and June,
the Piccolo Spoleto Festival. Tourists come from all over the world to
enjoy the arts and entertainment, which features world-renowned art-
ists. It is truly a magnificent two-week festival; so many organize their
schedules around it. One of the venues that was popular but no longer
operates during the festival was called The Coconut Club. It was a music
club that brought in acts from all over the country. Jazz, country, rock,
blues, diva singers, opera stars, and more contemporary local acts were
continuously performing their shows. There were as many as three to
four performances per night. Local folks were heavily involved at all
the venues, volunteering their time to help everything run smoothly.

It seemed like almost every beautiful lady living in the Lowcountry
would stop by The Coconut Club several times during the two weeks
to enjoy themselves. Guess who the volunteer maître d' was from
1989 through 1992? Great guess!

It was the perfect volunteer situation for a bachelor from Worcester, Massachusetts. For free drinks and food, I was at the women's beck and call. It was tough work. I even made business cards in case someone needed me for after-hours services. In other words, I was in the middle of Charleston's hip-hop scene and loved every minute of it. I could not have enjoyed myself any more than I did.

This gig led me to another gig that was just as much fun. Every year a group that was involved with the nonprofit organization March of Dimes put on a major fundraiser at the Omni Hotel, which now goes by the name of Charleston Place. The event was called Bid for Bachelors. I received an invitation to participate as one of the bachelors in 1992. My terribly busy schedule did not stop me from accepting the invitation. Did anyone think I would turn it down?

Twenty-two bachelors were selected. There were two smaller events leading up to the big day, but they weren't really that small. There was an open house at a nice downtown restaurant two weeks before the auction at the Omni Hotel. It was being promoted as a meet and greet for the single ladies to get to know Charleston's most popular bachelors (even as I write about this twenty-eight years later, I'm ready to fall out of my chair laughing). I decided to be a good sport and give out my personal cards upon request (*wink*).

The other lead-up social was a booze cruise that anyone could pay to go on and thus have a chance to get to know the bachelors. Now, before you think people did not get too caught up with this, think again. On the day of the Bid for Bachelors at the Omni, there was some serious money spent to go on a specially organized date with a bachelor. Several dates with bachelors were sold for well over one thousand dollars, with every penny going toward March of Dimes.

The date package I put together was a private sail for three hours on the Edisto River near Kiawah Island. Dinner was a Hawaiian luau on Kiawah Island. I went with my buddy Dennis, and it became a double date. Whoever bid on Dennis would be part of the date package I had put together, which included a ride in a stretch limo back and forth to Kiawah. Dennis sold for $550, and I sold for $375. Halfway through the date, Dennis and his new young lady friend wanted to leave and go to his home because they had decided they were going to get married. I hope nobody thinks I'm making this up. They have been married for twenty-seven years and are the proud parents of two daughters. My date went well, but I never told her that she didn't have to spend her money to date me. I would have been delighted to take her along for free. We only dated a couple more times afterward.

A bizarre situation took place on my way out of the Omni at the end of the event. When you walked into the ballroom, there were life-size posters with a different bachelor on each one. I was planning to take mine home and send it to Brooke and Karli because I knew they would get a kick out of seeing it. The problem was a lady ahead of me was leaving and taking mine home with her. I caught up with her and asked if I could have mine to give to my daughters in Massachusetts. She would not give it to me. I pleaded with her, and she still would not budge. The crazy part is she wasn't even interested in having a conversation with me. She barely talked with me. All she wanted was my life-size poster. The next weekend I went down to the market district by myself. A lady approached me and mentioned that her friend had my poster from the bachelor fundraiser. I asked her if she could ask her friend for it, so I could give it to my daughters. She told me her friend wasn't willing to part with it. To this day I seriously cannot figure out any of it. I remain disappointed my daughters never got to see my poster. I certainly hope the lady with my poster enjoyed waking up each morning looking at her favorite bachelor.

I started frequenting the night spots in downtown Charleston, and there were many. I found myself heading down to the weekend party district of East Bay Street and Market Street in downtown Charleston every Friday and Saturday night. There were several clubs that were packed on weekends in the late eighties and early nineties in Charleston. I was enjoying being a swinging single in the South.

I was not interested in a serious relationship. I was looking to meet single women and have a couple of drinks and a good time. It was a great time to be single in Charleston, that's for sure. My favorite night spots during those days were Henry's, Juke Box, Miskins, and Cumberland's. I was developing all kinds of problems for myself. I became good at having fun and walking away.

The partying nightlife can be a dangerous one to get caught up in. Just to set the record straight, I have never or would never allow myself to use any sort of drugs or let myself be anywhere near where they were being used. I was always proud of the condition I kept myself in, and as a high school counselor I continually tried to steer all my students away from any type of addictive behavior.

I was starting to enjoy beer and alcohol way more than I should have, though. I was taking advantage of being a bachelor. After a couple of years, I was starting to not like myself. Remember, I had two young daughters, and I wanted to have them proud of me. I wasn't proud of myself. Also, I knew I couldn't keep up with this lifestyle, or I was going to be facing consequences that would be long-lasting.

My last word about drinking. Today I seldom ever have more than one beer or one mixed drink. There is absolutely nothing wrong with drinking when people do it in moderation. It bothers me when I attend a social function and people look at those without a drink with a puzzled look on their faces like, why are these people not being social. I know I can have fun without any, or just one or two. When it's getting very late and I'm at a social function and I see that alcohol is still flowing, I usually start removing myself because absolutely nothing good is going to come of it.

Thirteen

THE DAY MY LIFE RESTARTED

I've got nowhere left to hide
It looks like love has finally found me
—FOREIGNER, "I WANT TO KNOW WHAT LOVE IS"

It was Friday evening, March 7, when I decided to stop by Henry's Club and Restaurant on Market Street after I had been to a college basketball game at the North Charleston Coliseum. It was around 11:00 p.m. when I saw two beautiful ladies sitting at a small table by themselves. I walked over and asked if they would like a drink. When I delivered their drinks, I was invited to sit down and enjoy a conversation. After the introductions, I couldn't even talk. All that came out of my mouth was "Do you like basketball?"

I had met the love of my life. The brown-haired, hazel-eyed beautiful lady with a gorgeous smile became my constant partner after that brief introduction in everything I have done and will do going forward. Thank goodness my bachelor days came to an abrupt halt. I was finally ready to have a serious relationship with a sweet and beautiful woman.

Barbara Lindsay had just gotten out of an unhappy marriage; her divorce was quite difficult. She had two children, and when children are involved in any divorce, it puts a tremendous amount of strain on both parents and the children. We dated for several years. I had several commitments and my daughters had me traveling to Massachusetts quite frequently.

The nice part for Barbara and me was that I had met her a couple of months before I graduated from the Citadel, and she was in her first course in the same program there. It was a convenient coincidence.

We enjoy the same lifestyle and have a great time together. We are always going out enjoying ourselves. Barbara remains to this day the sweetest, brightest, and most generous person I have ever met. She graduated from the University of South Carolina with a degree in education and was a teacher in Charleston directly thereafter. Neither of us ever tried to bring our children together as one family, although later Brooke and Barbara's daughter Lindsay became great friends.

We got married in August of 1996. I immediately sold my home in Shadowmoss and moved into Barbara's beautiful home in Mount Pleasant. It was a beautiful wedding with our friends and family at the Charleston Yacht Club. After Barbara received her master's at the Citadel, we were for many years the only husband and wife couple that were both counselors in the Charleston County School District. Barbara was at the middle school level, and I was at the high school level. I have always said I was the second-best school counselor in our family.

Barbara Epstein has an energy level like no one else. She never stops. She is an incredible grandmother to the seven grandchildren that we share. Her hobbies include cooking, working in her garden, and being a mom, a handyman, and a knitter. Barbara has an identical twin sister. Their personalities are similar, but it ends there. Tricia is also quite nice and multitalented. They both love riding horses on Tricia's ranch outside of Charleston. I am pleased that they get along so well. They are a fantastic support system for each other.

Barbara and I have been blessed to have had the opportunity to travel all over America and Europe. We enjoy the West Coast and have spent a great deal of time in Sedona, Arizona, and Lake Tahoe,

Nevada. We also spend a great amount of time in the summers on Cape Cod. Barbara has become a huge Red Sox fan and a fan of whatever basketball team I am coaching. Remember, I asked her if she liked basketball when I met her. Well, she had never been to a game in her life. Holy cow, whenever my team loses a game, she will let me know that she isn't happy with the result. The best thing about Barbara is she has my back. I have organized and promoted several events over the years, and with her around, I know no one will try and take advantage of me and my generosity. My generosity has been a problem for me throughout the years. I have never learned to say the word "no." We recently celebrated our twenty-fourth anniversary (they said it couldn't be done) and are already planning a Yellowstone vacation for our twenty-fifth next year.

Fourteen

JAMES ISLAND HIGH TROJANS, 1993–2001

Working at James Island High School (JIHS) in Charleston County School District was my dream job. What a tremendous opportunity it was to be able to have my first guidance counselor position at James Island.

James Island is a wonderful neighborhood community. It is located just on the outskirts of Charleston, on the way to Folly Beach. It has its own rich history dating back to the Revolutionary War. The high school has its own history. In the seventies and eighties, there were two high schools on the island. Fort Johnson High and JIHS combined to become one high school in 1985. The community does a fantastic job of supporting its high school. The spirit in the community, as well as the school, is in a league of its own. As an educator you don't have to work to build school spirit. It is already there waiting to explode at every opportunity.

The northern explosion of Charleston had not yet taken place in the nineties when I was there. Everyone on the island was like one big family. The natives had gone to one of the two high schools while growing up and wore their pride on their sleeves.

The faculty was extraordinary. It was an older, experienced faculty. There was little turnover from year to year. Once you got on the faculty, you most likely never wanted to leave. I always felt the principal set the tone for the school.

Floyd Hiott was a truly kind and generous man. Everyone wanted to pitch in and do their part in helping the students succeed. It is important to understand that some people may have thought he was a little too soft. That wasn't the case at all. Mr. Hiott could be as tough as he needed to be. In fact, you didn't want to ever be in a situation where you saw that side, though such situations didn't happen often.

My relationship with Floyd was immediately a positive one. We were able to confide in each other about almost everything. There have been two principals in my career whom I have trusted, and Mr. Hiott was absolutely one of them. He was like a big brother to me. The reason I felt close to him was because his personality was a lot like my own dad's. Several people on the faculty knew how close I was with my dad and even asked me a few times if Floyd reminded me of my dad. The answer was yes, he did.

My favorite memory of Mr. Floyd Hiott is that on every Friday afternoon, after the students were released, he would get on the intercom and announce the following: "Teachers, I just got a phone call from the bug man on top of the Wapoo Bridge on James Island, and he'll be here in ten minutes. Everyone must leave the building and go home now!" How could you not love the guy?

During all eight years of my tenure, I was given the assignment to work with the ninth and tenth graders. I was also the school's testing coordinator and Red Ribbon consultant.

There were on the average about fifteen to sixteen hundred students attending every year during my eight-year stay. The students for the most part had great relationships with most of the faculty. I found most of the students to be motivated towards their academics.

James Island High was one of the first high schools in South Carolina to incorporate the International Baccalaureate curriculum into its course of studies. IB learners strive to be thinkers, communicators, reflective, open minded, risk takers, caring and knowledgeable all within a global community.

I was already concerned about the dropout situation based on my years as the teacher of the High School Eight program at NCHS. Early on I noticed that this could also be a problem at James Island, which surprised me greatly. I was starting to realize that the dropout situation was a problem at every school in every state across America in the 1990s.

The sports programs at JIHS were exceptionally good. The football and baseball programs had a rich tradition. The student and community support for all the athletic teams were without a doubt the best of any of the schools I ended up working at in Charleston County.

The men's basketball program was in the middle of a great run of success. A new young hardworking coach had started in the late eighties and had discovered a gold mine of talented players led by a young man named Chuckie Robinson. Remember, I had started my career at James Island when I first moved to Charleston. My basketball background had helped open several doors for me in the school system. This, I thought, was also the case with Mr. Hiott when he hired me the first time in January of 1989.

Before I came back to James Island the second time, I had already served as an assistant basketball coach for two seasons under Head Coach Ronnie Dupre. Coach Dupre really loved the game and did a fantastic job of teaching it.

Chuckie Robinson grew up in the projects of James Island. He was a six-foot-seven ball of energy when we first met. His potential was off the charts. He was having a hard time getting reeled in. There were a few conflicts between the head coach and Chuckie. Chuckie wasn't sure he was going to be able to trust me in the beginning, until we started playing one-on-one after practices. It was during these games that I gained Chuckie's respect, and from there our friendship took off.

I'm proud of Chuckie. He went off to a junior college in Texas after leaving James Island. From there he went to East Carolina University, where he played his final two seasons. Chuckie had a sensational senior season and was the MVP of the Maui Classic. Chuckie would go on to have a seventeen-year professional career playing in Argentina. He has become a great husband, dad, and now grandfather. We remain extremely close. Every year he calls me on Father's Day. We attend each other's special family events. Chuckie and a few of his classmates—namely, Jermaine Scott and Jackie Simmons—combined to make James Island a basketball powerhouse. JIHS won a SC State AAAA Basketball Championship and lost by one point in the final game another year with this core of players. Even for many years after these three players were gone the program flourished. My supervisor in the guidance department at JIHS kept me on a close leash and wouldn't allow me to coach.

One of my biggest challenges was trying to help the ninth graders and tenth graders mature when it came to their academics. This is a universal situation. Many times, young teenagers come into a high school setting with poor study skills. They have just left a middle school where they didn't have to work really hard to succeed. They now get into a high school curriculum, taking algebra, physical science, world geography, and either Spanish or French, and what do you know—their grades drop, and the parents panic.

Parents want answers as to why their little Johnny and cute little Mary aren't bringing home A's anymore. It's about the following formula for success. *The M&M formula for success!*

For many years I have wanted to put a trademark on this formula. I think I developed this formula thinking about my own academic struggles in my youth. For young people to be *motivated* about their academics, they also must be *mature*. Without either one of these two characteristics, they are going to struggle. What I point out to parents who are looking for answers is this: We can talk, talk, talk, and then talk some more, but without self-motivation, we can talk forever. I believe that the trigger for self-motivation is growing up and maturing.

The problem with this formula is many times the parents and educators are waiting and holding their breath for the maturity to finally kick in. Whenever it happens, watch out because that young person often explodes in front of everyone's eyes. That is why it is so important for everyone to never quit on anyone at any age.

I have been teaching this formula for success throughout my entire career. I've taken it everywhere with me, and I plan on taking this formula for success to my grave.

Never forget Pathfinder's famous formula for success: *maturity and motivation equal success*! It's about the M&Ms! No maturity and motivation equal no *candy*!

One of the beautiful things about James Island was its diversity. It was awesome. There were few disciplinary problems for a school its size. Everyone for the most part got along well. The school had its typical problems. Hats being worn in the building and beer drinking and weed smoking at weekend parties. Those truancy meetings, though, I just couldn't shake. They gave me nightmares. I could not wrap my head around why young people would drop out of school before graduating.

This was about the time I started to wonder if South Carolina might have a hole in its education system. Why not move the dropout age from seventeen to eighteen if in fact we are losing students to the street because they are too immature and unmotivated to make good decisions? It remains an ongoing dilemma that has bothered me well into my retirement. I regularly see my former students from James Island around town. I enjoy seeing how so many have their own families and have become successful professionals. A few I still worry about.

The program that I am most proud of when I was at JIHS is the Olympic Torch Run. Red Ribbon awareness is about educating students about the dangers of alcohol and drug use. The year of the Olympic Games in nearby Georgia in 1996, I decided to take advantage of the excitement. The prom season can be a dangerous time for young people who are excited about having a memorable night.

State Farm Insurance had created a contest among all 150 high schools in South Carolina. It was called the Prom Promise Campaign.

I knew of the whereabouts of the Olympic torch that had been used to light the flame at the 1984 Olympic Games in Los Angles. It was sitting in a display case on the campus of the Citadel. If the Citadel would only allow me to borrow it, the students would be in for a special treat. The Citadel agreed to it.

All the elementary and middle schools on James Island organized school-wide assemblies. There are seven total public schools located on James Island. Several students from each of the seven schools would run to each school with police escorts. The schools were separated by not more than one mile. When the students reached a given school, one of them would run around the gym holding the Olympic torch high over their head while the entire student body cheered like crazy.

Now for the Red Ribbon part. The students were joined on the run by famous professional athletes, well-known TV personalities, and Ms. and Mrs. South Carolina. Remember, I like pretty girls! When we arrived at a school's gym to waiting students, we would then conduct a drug and alcohol awareness program. The celebrities and a few students would be the speakers. When the assembly ended, all the students would go back to their classes and sign Prom Promise pledge cards promising not to drink and drive. The celebrities and a few students were off to the next school escorted by blaring sirens, with the lead runner holding the Olympic torch!

What school do you think won the State Farm Prom Promise Campaign in South Carolina? The winner's check of $5,000 was presented to my main man, Mr. Floyd Hiott. I just loved that guy. I would have stayed forever if he hadn't retired.

With a new principal, everything at JIHS changed quickly. It wasn't as much fun to be a Trojan anymore. The thing I remember about my four years with our new principal was her fat, little Jack Russell that would follow her around school all day. The mutt reminded me of a fat, little gerbil.

It was perfect timing for a new school to open in Charleston—and for a phone call from that school's new principal.

Fifteen

WEST ASHLEY HIGH WILDCATS, 2001–2011

The phone call from Mr. Bob Olson could not have come at a better time. I was starting to get antsy at James Island. There was no way I could find another JIHS, but I just wasn't feeling comfortable anymore.

I had known Bob since just after I moved to Charleston. Bob and I would often attend sporting events together. I knew Mr. Olson to be a fair man whom I could comfortably work with. Mr Olson also offered Ronnie Dupre a job in the math department and as the men's varsity basketball coach. It was nice for me to have someone that I already had a working relationship with transferring with me.

The school that Bob had spent over a year designing with the contractors was to be called West Ashley High School (WAHS). He offered me the positions of career counselor and JV basketball coach. It took me less than two and a half seconds to accept his offer. I was now a Wildcat!

The first time I ever saw the campus, I just about fainted. It was incredible, amazing. I had no idea that it was one of the first state-of-the-art campuses to be opened in the twenty-first century in South Carolina.

The Campus is located off a major highway called Glenn McConnell Highway, in the West Ashley section of Charleston. To get to the campus you need to leave the highway and then drive over a half-mile to get to the school. West Ashley High is in such a setting that students were not able to walk to school. Because of recent construction developments around the campus West Ashley High now is part of a neighborhood. When West Ashley first opened and for many years later some students were not able to attend after school programs because they lacked transportation. This situation held the school spirit back quite a bit.

It was so exciting to be given one of the guidance offices to work out of. Now, for the best part of the campus in my opinion. I have been in basketball gyms at both the high school and college level my whole life, but when I walked into the new Wildcat Basketball Arena, I thought my heart had stopped. I have never once called it a gym. The Wildcat Arena had seating capacity for a little over two thousand people. It was the colors that jumped right out at me. West Ashley had taken the nickname "Wildcats," the same one adopted by Kansas State University. That was not all that West Ashley had borrowed. We had the same color schemes of black and my favorite color, purple. We even had the Kansas State University logo. I felt we were Kansas State reincarnated as a high school in South Carolina.

Another part of the fifty-two-million-dollar campus was a magnificent, comprehensive state-of-the-art music, art and performing arts center. The instructors for this department, Ellyn Winkles and Nancy Shurlds, were two of the most popular teachers on the Wildcat staff.

I was all pumped up for the start of school, and so was the rest of the faculty. We were going to be given the opportunity to open a high school campus that the Charleston County School District had just spent fifty-two million dollars to build. I was in seventh heaven.

When WAHS opened, the campuses of Middleton High and St. Andrews High both closed. These two schools had been fierce rivals on the playing fields for many years. What people didn't know was that the two feeder neighborhoods for Middleton and St. Andrew's also had a different kind of rivalry. This rivalry of gangs caused a problem during that first year. I am going to talk more about that situation later.

As a career counselor, it was my responsibility to help all the students explore their career paths. Out into the community I happily went. I literally knocked on the doors of every major business in Charleston County looking for both speakers and mentors to come to Wildcat country to work with our students. We developed some fantastic business partners, who became invaluable to the Wildcats throughout the years. Through this effort I met a group of businessmen who would become my friends. It was a win-win situation for everyone. Classroom presentations of career information were ongoing throughout my ten years at WAHS.

A career counselor at a school is also responsible for the development of the career curriculum that students select their courses from. To draft this curriculum, we developed a team with Ms. Mary Runyon, who was our assistant principal and who in 2006 took over from Bob Olson as the principal, and Ms. Sandy Pennekamp, who served as the career technology education (CTE) chairperson.

They were absolutely the best professionals of all time to work with. They each became more like sisters to me. We were perfect complements to each other. Plus, we had a blast working together. Sandy had a fantastic sense of humor and had my back every time I screwed up, and there were many of those occasions.

The curriculum gave each student an opportunity to select a major within the CTE curriculum. Examples include comprehensive study of accounting, computer technology, health sciences, pre-engineering, fine arts, marketing along with others.

The Lowcountry is home to one of the finest two-year technical community colleges in the country. Throughout my entire career, I leaned on Trident Tech heavily to help support our students' career goals. There wasn't a week that went by during my twenty-seven-year career that I wasn't in contact with the Trident faculty, who would come to the different schools I worked at and meet with the students.

It would be impossible for me to remember how many times I took field trips to Trident with my students so they could visit the campus and explore all that the school had to offer.

Mary and Sandy were the brains of our team (thank goodness) and did an amazing job of creating new CTE courses and majors continuously. My job within the team was to hustle around to all the classes and students on campus and share the course offerings. We worked great together. One year the entire CTE Department at West Ashley was given the prestigious award of Career Technology School of the Year in South Carolina for the 2002–2003 school year.

Part of what we were doing, before any other school in Charleston County, was allowing our students to be transported during the day to Garrett Academy. Garrett Academy is a four-year career-vocational high school located in North Charleston. Students from WAHS could now take a two-credit career course without being full-time students at Garrett. Before this, if a student didn't enroll at Garrett out of eighth grade, they were completely shut out of all opportunities available on Garrett's campus during their high school years. West Ashley pursued funds from the district office after a certain career counselor spent a few years begging and crying out for this added funding. It all went back to my years at Boys' Trade and remembering how much that vocational education had helped so many of my friends. Welding, masonry, auto body repair, and other trades now became part of the WAHS curriculum.

As I write this book, there is construction going on at the campus of WAHS in front of the football stadium. A building geared toward all the state-of-the-art career technology and vocational opportunities will be available for every student. The building is set to open for the start of the 2021–2022 school year. The day the West Ashley Center for Advanced Studies opens, a big cheer should go up for two retired education leaders. Without the vison and perseverance of Ms. Runyon and Ms. Pennekamp, this invaluable addition to the Wildcat campus would never have become a reality.

Once again, though, I was concerned with how many young students were dropping out of the system before graduation. After I was at WAHS for a few years, the State Department became aware of this national dropout crisis. Students started to get tracked more closely by the attendance office and all the school's administrators. A comprehensive credit recovery program was also put into place to give any student who might be struggling a chance to catch up and regain a credit for a class they might be failing or had already failed.

It was finally happening at the state level. The high schools in South Carolina were receiving the help needed to hand out more diplomas and improve the dropout rate.

This is where I want to get back to the discipline problems that impacted West Ashley High. I feel terrible that I must address this issue at all because I have so many friends who have given their blood, sweat, and tears to make WAHS a fantastic school.

The problem of rival neighborhood gangs developed when WAHS first opened in 2001. After about a year to a year and a half, the problem was under control. The aftershocks have been felt for several years after, however. The perception formed during those early years has been extremely hard to shake. It is totally unfair that at times Wildcat country has had to carry a false perception longer than it should have.

Let me set the record straight. If my daughters Brooke and Karli had grown up in Charleston, I would have been thrilled to see them graduate from WAHS. I feel the same way about my granddaughters today. West Ashley High does a tremendous job of offering a large selection of honor, dual credit, and advance placement courses. False and old perceptions can be brutal to shake.

The sports programs have had their ups and downs. Early on the girls' programs experienced a lot of success. The Lady Wildcats won the state championship in both soccer and volleyball.

The men's basketball program has been the only consistent winner in boys' sports since the school opened. That first year in 2001-2002 my long-time coaching colleague Ronnie Dupre who was the head coach and I led the Wildcats to a conference championship and twenty-two wins. Terrell Everett, who was a senior, was a one-man wrecking crew for us that first year. Terrell went on to a sensational career at the University of Oklahoma and is still playing in Europe. Looking back, I realize winning games was not the biggest challenge we had as coaches. Overcoming the apathy within the Wildcat athletic program was going to be something we would have to deal with for many years.

Wrestling, track, and tennis have had several outstanding individual athletes competing at different times. Football has struggled to establish a winning tradition. There is no question that during the first few years of the school, the old rivalries held football back a bit. Rivalries and perceptions die hard.

At this time, I'm going to address what almost all counselors I have worked with have had to deal with. Every school I have worked at has had an incredible number of amazing students. Many students earn scholarship opportunities that can take them to some of the best colleges in America. Here becomes a little bit of the situation.

South Carolina has some fine colleges: Clemson, Coastal Carolina, the University of South Carolina, and the College of Charleston are just a few of the state-run universities in South Carolina. College athletic rivalries are extremely popular among the high school students. Many parents have attended these rival schools. With the excitement these colleges create, some young children decide at an early age they want to continue the family legacy and take part in the exciting Saturdays at their state universities.

I will explain here what happens in every state all over America; it's a commonplace situation. Some high school seniors bypass scholarship opportunities at schools outside of their home states that possibly could be the start of better opportunities they may never have known existed. It usually works out well for everyone, including the families, when students remain in state, but students can always come back to their home state and continue to cheer for the rest of their lives, while their college educational experience only lasts usually about four years.

I wouldn't call this situation a problem. At different times my counseling colleagues and I got a little frustrated when an Ivy League university or another of America's top universities scholarship opportunity gets passed over to attend a college in state.

Sixteen

St. John's High, 2011–2014

I t was about mid-April, and I received a phone call around eleven in the morning in my office. It was Lee Runyon, Mary's son, who was in his first year as the principal of St. John's High on John's Island.

Mr. Runyon offered me a terrific opportunity to become the counselor for boys at St. John's, as well as the varsity boys' basketball coach. This is just the introduction to what was the most bizarre situation I have found myself in during my entire twenty-seven-year career in the Charleston County School District.

Please understand something here. I accepted the job as basketball coach over ten times, and each time the St. John's community pressured the school board to renege on the offer. If anyone thinks I might be exaggerating, well, I wish I were.

Lee Runyon did absolutely nothing wrong by offering me the coaching position. Every principal has the right to hire the coach he wants.

Yet the community on John's Island was trying to take control of the school, and I got caught right in the middle. The community didn't know me yet; I was just a name to its members at the time. They wanted me to come to St. John's as the boys' counselor, but they didn't want me to coach. I had been offered both positions, and I wasn't willing to transfer schools if the jobs weren't packaged together. The crazy thing about this tug-of-war was that it went on for five months, right up until the very first day of school.

The human resources office for CCSD screwed up also and had me sign two different contracts at two different schools. On the first day of the school year, when my alarm went off, I didn't know what school I was going to be working at. I could have reported to either St. John's High or WAHS. Until I got in my car and drove to the end of my street, I didn't know if I was turning left toward West Ashley or right toward St. John's. No one had any idea what I was going to do because I didn't know. Neither Lee Runyon nor Mary Runyon knew that morning which school I was going to show up at. All I knew was I had a job somewhere for the 2011–2012 school year. This is 100 percent the truth.

When I got to the end of the road, I stopped. I thought for about thirty seconds and said to myself, *I'm ready for a new challenge; let's go right.*

Do I think a couple of people were screwing with me? Absolutely!

It was a power struggle over a couple factors. I mentioned one factor, but there is another that I refuse to get into publicly. The only thing I'll say is that it had nothing to do with my reputation as a professional. Here is what I know—as soon as I got out to St. John's on the very first day, I was given the royal treatment. The community of John's Island became a giant-size family for me. I have never had more fun with a student body over the course of my career. The kids and the parents on this rural island outside of Charleston were a dream to work with. The student population of St. John's High is mostly Black, with a few Hispanic students mixed in.

As far as coaching basketball, they had decided as a group to go in a different direction before I got there, and their reward was mud all over their faces. I got over not coaching quickly, but the students and many parents became furious about how I had been treated after getting to know me and tried to have me become their coach after they had already hired one. It's all good; I had made the right decision and was ready for my next chapter in my career.

Lee Runyon and I worked incredibly well together. It was a fantastic three-year run.

St. John's is a Title I school, meaning most of the student body is on free or reduced cost lunch. During the three years I worked at St. John's, the school was given a three-year federal grant to hire extra support staff. The dropout rate was high at the time, and with this extra support, the community and the school district were hoping for positive results.

The cohort of added teacher-coaches and educators consisted of Sandy Brossard, Lynn Clegg, Kathy Gehr, and a few others. Will someone please tell me why women are all so smart? They were incredible. They could pull data apart and analyze the results more quickly and more accurately than I have ever seen. When it came to student decision-making, they left me speechless, which is extremely hard to do.

Lee Runyon led a charge of turning the academics around in a big way. With the grant, the faculty and the students improved the dropout rate by over 30 percent. For a student body of under three hundred, that is tremendous.

Perceptions are tough to deal with and really hit a nerve with me. When I was at St. John's, we had fewer problems than at any school I had ever worked at. No, it had nothing to do with the size of the school. It was because a pride of growing up on the island and continuing the legacy of their family members who had also attended St. John's was important to our students.

For the first time, I could really see how effective the credit recovery programs were in decreasing the dropout rate. If used properly and not manipulated by the school or the students, they could make a huge difference. The only problem with the programs was that some students took advantage of them and thus learned to become manipulative later in life. St. John's used them wonderfully, though.

My whole focus on working with students is *hope*! Students need to feel like they are leaving high school with *hope*! Diplomas are wonderful, but if a student doesn't have a sense of hope to go along with it, what good does the diploma do? I'm a stickler on this. That's why career and vocational education courses can be a student's life blood. Unfortunately, there is still a stigma out there among some people that if you don't get a college education, you are not going be successful.

A drawback of growing up in a rural area can be lack of access and exposure to several opportunities that someone from a big city might have. Also, small high schools such as St. John's are not able to offer as many diverse academic opportunities as a high school like West Ashley High. Lee Runyon and I made sure when we were out on the island that this situation was not going to be a drawback for our students.

We had the largest collection of speakers and business partners coming to and going from the home of the Islanders all day long. Every single day classes had speakers and mentors stopping by. Even though we were a small, rural school, we brought in the biggest names in every walk of life we could recruit. Whom do you think was given the responsibility to recruit these professionals? How did you guess?

We had CEOs from *Fortune* 500 companies, along with TV news anchors, professional athletes, government leaders, and even a world-renowned African peacekeeper named Aki Stavrou. It was a who's who of America coming through our doors on the Island. I hope you didn't think our students were going to be left out of meeting highly well-known and very famous successful professionals, did you?

The list of speakers included Jim Stuckey and Travis Jervey, who had both won Super Bowls. Among the other NFL players to stop by were Langston Moore and Terry Cousin. NBA all-stars Michael Adams and Xavier McDaniel both loved hanging out with our students and teaching life lessons and motivating. Senator Marlon Kimpson and CEO Anita Zucker both spent time in our school. College basketball coaches Al Skinner (also an NBA star), Bobby Cremins, and Les Robinson were also guests. The general manager of the South Carolina Ports Authority, Jim Young, and Brad Davis, owner of Rick Hendricks BMW in Charleston, were extremely active business partners. Once again, I must remind the readers here that St. John's High is located out in the boondocks.

One of my proudest moments was when our speaker-mentor program was featured by my buddy Gene Sapakoff, who is the feature sports columnist for the Charleston *Post and Courier* daily regional newspaper. His published article was genuinely nice and well appreciated by everyone on the island, but what came out of it shocked everyone.

The national, well-read magazine *Coach* found the article online and featured little St. John's High on its preseason football cover with a four-page feature on our speaker-mentor program at the start of the 2014 college and NFL football seasons.

We even took field trips so our students could visit college campuses all over the southeastern United States. Though we made significant efforts to boost college admission scores among our students, unfortunately they were never able to make significant improvement in this area. This is why I feel the SAT and ACT exams have a racial bias to them. People have a right to disagree with me all they want, but I've seen it up close. We held several workshops to help our juniors and seniors get over this hurdle, but regardless of how much effort they put into it, some just could not improve to the level that they needed to reach in order to gain admission to some of the better colleges. I'm not saying every student had this problem, but it was more prevalent than we wanted it to be. It was frustrating for everyone, including the parents.

The faculty at St. John's High was extraordinary. What a hardworking, dedicated staff. If people could only watch our professional educators work for a day or a week, they would walk away marveling at their level of commitment. Some of the most unsung heroes on a staff include counselors and psychologists. St. John's High has a couple of the finest I have ever worked with.

Carrie Rittle was in a league of her own as a Charleston County School District psychologist. She was not just there to test students for special needs, but she was also hands-on with all the students. I don't know what I would have done without her. We had worked together for a few years at WAHS, so when we both got to St. John's, we were already exceptionally good friends. We made a tremendous team. I'm not going to say she was like my assistant because I leaned on her as much as she leaned on me for a lot of our decision-making. We used to say that we knew exactly what the other person was thinking by just looking in each other's eyes. Carrie would continue to call me after I retired to have me stop by a school she was working at and meet with her students so she could consult with me.

My counseling colleague at St. John's was Brenda Jenkins. Ms. Brenda has one of the biggest hearts for young people of anyone I have ever worked with. Just extraordinary.

Some counselors get a bad reputation just because we don't work in a classroom as teachers. It is not fair! The workload a counselor has depends on the size of the student body. At St. John's I took half of the student body, which was less than two hundred students. When I worked at James Island, I had over six hundred students. At West Ashley I was the career counselor for the entire student body. The counselor is responsible for tracking each student in their workload by checking on the student's academic progress. Also, each student from the time they enter high school must meet regularly with their counselor to set up what is called an Individual Graduation Plan, commonly referred to as an IGP. This assures the student is taking courses that are relevant to his future career goals. With the responsibility of each student's emotional well-being and overall educational and personal growth on the counselor, the pressure can really become unbearable at times.

I have been lucky. I've only worked with a couple of counselors over the years who were not suited for the profession. Some counselors don't spend enough time outside their offices for my liking because of all the paperwork that is also part of the job. Many times, though, that isn't the fault of the counselors. We get a lot of extra stuff piled on us by administrators. It becomes extremely hard to juggle all the hats we are constantly asked to wear. That's why my working friendship with Ms. Rittle was so helpful; we both really understood the pressure of the job.

Some of my favorite memories of education come from my work at St. John's High. Reverend Dr. Eric Mack is currently the chairman of the Charleston County School Board. He is a business and educational leader on John's Island. I became friendly with Rev. Mack and his family. His son was my student for the three years I was on the Island.

Several times over the last few years, Rev. Mack has had me as his guest at his church in downtown Charleston, Bethany Baptist. The church has a predominantly African American congregation. During the three visits I have made to the church, I have felt as comfortable as when I attend a Jewish temple. I have been asked to speak to the congregation on each occasion and have even been asked to honor the congregation's war veterans on Veterans Day. I also received a special engraved pen to use when the dropout age bill I am seeking to change in South Carolina gets passed. Every time I am invited, it's a big thrill for me. Barbara has also attended along with me. What a beautiful world this has a chance to be some day.

Whenever I go back to John's Island or travel out to Kiawah Island, I always drive by the basketball court that I asked the County of Charleston to build less than a half a mile from where the high school is located. Whenever I move to a new community for work, I drive around the neighborhoods to make sure there is a basketball court available for public use. On my first day of work on John's Island, when I drove around the Island, I didn't see one. I called Tom O'Rourke, the Director of the Charleston County Parks Department. We set up a meeting with Lee Runyon.

I remain very proud to know that John's Island has one of the most beautiful state-of-the-art outdoor basketball facilities I have ever seen. Barbara and I also bought a large mural for the school when I left, which shows the colors and pride of the Islanders.

What started as a difficult transfer situation turned into the most memorable three years I ever had anywhere. My boys are no longer boys, but I feel very confident they left St. John's High with the *hope* and educational skills needed to go out and make John's Island very proud of the men they will continue to be.

Without a federal grant and without Rev. Mack on the school board monitoring funds, there always remains the danger of St. John's reverting back to the status of a low-performing school.

Seventeen

A WILDCAT AGAIN, THE LAST HURRAH 2014-2015

With the three-year federal grant coming to an end at St. John's, I knew my work there was over. My salary had come out of the grant. I knew my career was closing fast. I wasn't sure whether I had one year left in me or two. I was mentally going on fumes. In public education you must know when to walk away. I have seen so many educators hang on just to collect a paycheck. Once money becomes the sole reason for working, you become dead weight to the system, and the kids get screwed. The older educators are sometimes also afraid to walk away because they don't know of anything else, they can do.

Lee Runyon was going over to WAHS as principal to replace his mom, Mary Runyon. Mary was going to become the Charleston County School District's Director of Academic Curriculum. I received a call from Lee asking me if I would be willing to return to West Ashley with him. It was perfect timing. This was going to be a chance to be around several people I was comfortable working with and a chance to say some final goodbyes if I chose to retire.

My assignment was going to be working with students who had fallen behind academically or who were unmotivated. The maturity and motivation equal success formula was going to be put to the test one more time.

I knew exactly what I had to do, for two reasons. Number one, I had worked previously at West Ashley for ten years; the other reason was that I always could identify with the underdog.

West Ashley in an average year has a student enrollment of about seventeen hundred to eighteen hundred students. Over the years I have tried to limit my use of the term "at risk" since I have always believed that with all the social pressures a young person has to deal with today, all students can fall into the *at risk* category. My student workload count for students who were a couple of credits short of being in the right grade was a little more than three hundred.

I knew I was going to miss my main working colleague, Ms. Carrie Rittle, who had remained at St. John's. What I didn't know was that I was going to meet her clone, Suzannah Countryman. Suzannah was a former student of mine at James Island whom I remembered very well. "Suz" might have been a young psychologist, but like Carrie she had lots of savvy.

My office was located outside the school's guidance department, in the hall by the back entrance. This was fine with me. I am not sure I was ever a team player with my counselor colleagues. I'm just wired differently. I never tried hard to fit in. I cared more about being an agent for change.

It was great to be back as a Wildcat and spend time with the old gang. I wasn't working as closely with Sandy Pennekamp, the head of the CTE Department, but it was always nice to have her pop her head into my office a couple of times a week. We never had to say anything to each other to share a laugh. We both remembered how hysterical we would get at the monthly career education meetings we used to attend together downtown.

After meeting with most of the students on my list, I cut the number down to about one hundred who needed my support the most. Usually a student lacking only a credit or two will be all right with a little pep talk on my M&M formula.

Ms. Countryman and I knew there was a lot of work to do if we were going to try and help save so many young people. Right away, the first thing I knew I had to do was to track the attendance of the students in the group we would be working with. A student who falls behind by more than one year can become truant rather easily. The first thing that leaves such students is their motivation. When they become truant after turning seventeen, there isn't a single thing any-one, not even their parents, can do to get them to attend. It became my job to build their hope back up by finding reasons for them to want to attend. Sometimes it's a career or vocational class, a perform-ing arts class, ROTC, or maybe an extra physical education class. These students need more than just words. Floyd Hiott once told me, "By the time they have seen you, they have already heard everything from everyone." So true.

I decided to think out of the box and take a wild shot in the dark. We knew we needed a program to help support what we as a small team were going to try to do. This is when our team of two became a team of three. Ms. Liz Linda, an awesome special education teacher, joined our team. Suz, Liz, and I became a team of three and gave ourselves the name of "Team at Risk", we kept this name to ourselves.

I told my team members about my intention to reach out to Palmetto Goodwill Industry. Although I wasn't optimistic that Goodwill would be able to assist in our efforts to support our stu-dents, I felt the need to supplement West Ashley's campus vocational courses.

We contacted Palmetto Goodwill in North Charleston and set up a meeting with members of its staff. When we walked in, Suz and I were both surprised and pleased to see Goodwill had five of its top ad-ministrators waiting for us in their conference room. I had thought I was going to have to make one of my all-time best recruiting pitches. After my opening remarks, though, the director said, "Just tell us whatever you need us to do to support and train your students." Suz and I nearly fell out of our chairs. We had struck gold. Goodwill agreed to send one of its expert job skills trainers to West Ashley once a week to instruct the group of students on how to gain the necessary skills for employment.

This was the break our students needed. Not only did Goodwill supply its own curriculum and trainer, but there was also no cost to West Ashley. Lee Runyon almost fell over when we told him about this brand-new program that Goodwill said they had wanted to do for a long time but just didn't know how to get into CCSD. No problem—welcome aboard, Palmetto Goodwill.

Suz, Liz, and I invited thirty-three students to join the program. All the students were given parent permission forms to bring home, and all returned the signed forms for this cutting-edge program. A great benefit of the program, which lasted for twelve weeks, was that the students each received one elective credit upon completion. There was one other perk that all who completed the program would receive: the students would be given a paid part-time job at Goodwill. It was a win for all!

For a first-time program that had never been administered in any school in South Carolina, the Goodwill program was a huge success. I encouraged every high school in South Carolina to adopt this program. Unfortunately, as of now, no other school has taken advantage of this program for their students. It's a real shame. This program offered mentors, a trainer, internships, a high school credit, and paid jobs, but it came to a stop. Perhaps most administrators and counselors have such big caseloads it is hard to find the time to add one more program.

As the school year progressed, I shared the M&M formula for success inside every classroom whose teacher would give me access to speak to the students in their classes. Sadly, though, I knew that my career was finished. Nobody knew why. In a perfect world, I would have wanted one more year, but I had come to a complete stop. I was a sick man with a serious problem that had been ongoing for several months. I had been scared to tell anyone.

I wanted to give the students at WAHS one last hoorah from their eccentric counselor. I wanted it to be something the whole school would enjoy and never forget.

A professional sports day celebration was now on the calendar. On April 30, 2015, the home of the West Ashley High Wildcats would host an assembly for the entire school that would bring together the greatest group of professional athletes ever assembled at one time in any South Carolina school. One more big recruiting effort was now underway.

April 30th revealed an incredible array of stars on stage at West Ashley. My buddy, two-time Super Bowl Champion Jim Stuckey, was there. He was joined by two-time Olympic gold medalist and alumnus of old St. Andrew's High, Katrina McClain. World Series Champion Herm Winningham and NBA all-star Xavier McDaniel highlighted the event. Also attending were pro soccer players, pro golfers, famous basketball official Ted Valentine, and CBS sports analyst Debbie Antonelli, all of whom gave up their valuable time to tell us about their personal journeys and how they overcame obstacles to gain their stardom.

This pro athlete's day wasn't just one assembly. After the main assembly, every athlete in the school gathered with a coach in a classroom for a more informal question-and-answer session that gave everyone a chance to get up close to a professional star.

Everything went extremely well. We had an overflow of students in the assembly, and the coaches and student-athletes were thrilled to have a chance to meet pro athletes up close and have a photo opportunity with them. It was a thrilling day that I will always enjoy remembering.

Unfortunately, though, as wonderful as this event had been, as much as I loved working with these teachers and students, I had come to the realization that I was physically and emotionally finished. I was struggling badly. I couldn't stand up without holding onto a table or a chair or leaning against a wall. I was having dizzy spells ten to twelve times per day, in which if I didn't hold on, I would have fainted. My macho side kept waiting for them to go away. They didn't, but I didn't tell anyone, including Barbara.

After the assembly I spent the next month before school ended sitting in my office with the lights out and the door closed, so no one would think I was in.

West Ashley had a wonderful counselor who worked like I did. Perry Metz was always interacting with the entire student body and building relationships. I knew my students were going to be in good hands.

It was time to go home, get some rest, and hope that I would start feeling better so I could enjoy a long retirement. The last day of the school year came, and I turned in everything to the administration and checked out before the rest of the faculty. I couldn't say I was feeling sad.

I had some nice retirement events to look forward to. My guy Chuckie Robinson got a few of my former players together from James Island for a small dinner that last night. Bill Lynds was taking me to four Red Sox versus Braves games later that June. Two were in Boston, and then we would fly directly to Atlanta for two more the next day. My stepdaughter Lindsay and her husband Tommy took Barbara and me to Hall's Chop House in Charleston for dinner. I was also going to spend the entire month of July on Cape Cod at my favorite Falmouth Harbor cottage. It was all so genuinely nice.

At the end-of-the-year faculty meeting, on that last day before everyone went their own way, Mr. Runyon called up to the front of the auditorium everyone one by one who was not returning the next year. He called me up last. Hearing the response from the entire faculty remains one of the most special moments I have ever had. I wasn't expecting the reception I received.

I went back to my office for about thirty minutes so I could make myself available to some of my friends on the faculty that I had worked with for a total of eleven years. It was so nice for me to have an opportunity to say my final goodbyes. It was time to take my copy of the book *Black Like Me* home.

What an amazing group of students I had the chance to work with and coach over my twenty-seven-year career! I will never forget the experiences they gave me. Thank you to all!

What an amazing group of professionals, these folks I could call my colleagues.

Godspeed!

I had already called Barbara to tell her I was on my way home. When I walked to my car in the faculty parking lot, I had one last phone call to make.

I called my closest friend. When Brian Hammel out in Los Angeles picked up the phone, all this worn out counselor could say was, "Pathfinder is out."

West Ashley High is now under the leadership of Ryan Cumback. Mr Cumback will do a great job of leading Wildcat Nation. Ryan was a long-time teacher and assistant principal at West Ashley High before he became the principal. Ryan is young, hardworking, and extremely bright. Plus, he is constantly in motion and won't let anything interfere with the school's success.

Thank goodness my health returned with the help of a pacemaker. The pacemaker helped increase my heartrate to almost twice as fast as it had been before I retired.

The education system of South Carolina has come lightyears from the day I came on board in 1989. There have been so many advances made in reading literacy, CTE education, special education, mental health, and credit recovery programs that if there is a perception around America that our education system in South Carolina doesn't compare to the best, it is not accurate. Charleston County School District even has a high school, Academic Magnet, that was ranked as the number one public high school in America in 2019 by *U.S. News & World Report*.

Eighteen

AFRICA

B oth of my daughters attended and graduated from Northern Arizona University in Flagstaff. My youngest daughter, Karli, during her senior year decided to enroll in an international program that would take her to Ghana for a semester of studies. Once she was over there, a call came from Karli one Sunday afternoon with great excitement in her voice. "Dad, you've just got to come over to visit; it's beautiful, and we'll have so much fun together." So, as you have all figured out by now, I'm a big sucker for my girls. *Let's go!*

Another leave of absence for seven days during the fall of 2007 from WAHS was on my calendar. My principal, Mary Runyon, was good to me and knew if she gave me time off to accept certain invitations, I would develop a program for the school when I returned.

Ghana was a life changer. I spent ten days living in the University of Ghana guest quarters while hanging out with my daring daughter during the day.

All I can say is, *unbelievable!* The traveling we did together and the experiences we shared were absolutely life changing. Every American citizen should spend a week traveling the countryside villages of Africa to understand what poverty and homelessness really are. Most Americans have absolutely no idea. I have seen some stuff in my life, but nothing compares to what I experienced with my daughter—*absolutely nothing!* Africa makes the Middle East feel like paradise.

During my time over there, I had the two most amazing experiences of my life. In the town of Legon on the outskirts of the capital, Accra, is the country's major university. The facilities are beautiful but get ready if you step off the campus grounds. The open markets of the surrounding areas let you know right away that nothing in America can prepare you for the African lifestyle. Forget the photos; they do not come close to the real experience.

I enjoyed the people and the country landscape. Both are beautiful. Most Africans survive on just extremely basic needs of food, water, love, and shelter. Their food, water, and shelter are of a totally different standard, though. The level of poverty can be explained by the following example. Everywhere you went during the day, school-aged children would be on the side of the road selling fruit, water, or anything else their parents had given them to peddle when they had left home early in the morning. Homelessness in Africa has a different definition. Grab a blanket and lie down anywhere you think is safe. This is not considered homelessness. This is just the fact of life for many.

My first incredible experience came when Karli was in class. I did attend a couple of Karli's classes with her, until I started raising my hand and asking the professor questions, and then I was vetoed from attending anymore. There was a primary school just outside the campus that went from kindergarten to third grade. The front gate was protected around the clock by military guardsmen with loaded machine guns. Every time we went by the school, Karli could see me looking over my shoulder at it. My girl knew what I was thinking. Just before Karli went into her class, she warned me to stay away from the primary school as I could get into serious trouble. Well, kids aren't the only ones who don't listen too well; some parents don't either.

I did a beeline over to the primary school the moment Karli turned her back. When I approached the armed guards, I took a couple of hundred dollars out of my pocket and told the militia I wanted to donate money to the school. The guard in charge telephoned into the principal and asked her to come out. Sure enough, the head mistress came up to me, and we greeted each other. Then it was time to make my push to get behind the iron curtain. I explained I was an educator from America and wanted to make a generous donation to her school. I told her I just wanted to observe her students and teachers in their classes. My new head mistress friend was glad to accept my generous donation and walked me around her school and introduced me to every classroom. Then she told me to make myself at home and take whatever photos I wanted to. She also allowed for me to play with the kids at recess and to have lunch with them.

It was awesome. The kids in Africa are like kids everywhere—if they feel loved, they are happy. There was no question I was going to take advantage of this opportunity. In fact, I did read a story to over one hundred young children. We all had a big giant blast together.

The highlight of the trip to the primary school was when I got down and did push-ups for the kids. They were all going nuts counting until my arms gave out. This was when everyone started really going crazy. All the students and their teachers all got down and started doing push-ups while I counted.

The moral of this story is there is nothing to fear except fear itself. We are all put here for the same reason, and that is to experience love.

My next big adventure came when Karli took me on a fifty-mile taxi ride to the town of Cape Coast, Ghana. The Cape Coast Castle is the historical location where slaves were kept before they were put on boats that came directly to *Charleston*! The route of the journey was on a map hanging on the wall with Charleston highlighted as the destination.

The Cape Coast Castle might be considered a historic landmark, but it signifies one of the darkest historical events and periods known to mankind. Karli and I were given a tour of this museum, which sits on the shoreline of the Atlantic Ocean. Walking around the different rooms, the voices of echoes were crying out from every corner. When we stepped into the main dungeons, where the male slaves were kept in holding wearing shackles, my knees buckled on me. I got weak and almost fell. There I was in this twelve-by-twelve-foot dirt cellar of the Cape Coast Slave Castle looking out of a tiny opening in the wall just big enough for a little air. Over one hundred human beings were held in these small areas. Trenches were dug and used as toilets. When our tour guide told us, it was time to go visit the dungeon where the women were kept, I said I had already seen enough. What else was there to look at?

My little girl Karli had done me a huge favor. It was great to spend all that time with her, absolutely. Fun? I'm not so sure about the fun part. Did I learn a lot? *Oh my!*

When I returned home to WAHS, we started a big book drive for the primary school I had visited in Legon. We set our goal at five hundred books. After two weeks we shut our book drive down at five thousand books. We had run out of storage space. We found a sponsor to ship all the books to Ghana.

Wildcat strong, baby!

Nineteen

CHARLIE EPSTEIN DAY

'Cause my heart is broken in pieces
Yes, my heart is broken in pieces
Since you've been gone.
—GENESIS, "SINCE I LOST YOU"

It was 7:30 p.m. on Monday evening, November 29, 1999.

The perception I always had about Dad was that he was invincible and would live forever. I never gave a single thought to the fact I could lose Charlie Epstein from my life someday.

The phone rang. My sister Diane was calling to tell me Dad had just died. He had suffered an aneurysm rupture and had passed quickly. I had never experienced the level of grief that came over me. My entire life was shattered. Immediately I knew this could be something I would never get over. All I remember is I couldn't think or function. *Thank God* for Barbara. She just jumped in and took over my life. I was not unlike many other sons with their dads. I was devastated.

Dad and my brother, Bobby, had just visited with Barbara and me three weeks earlier at our home in Mount Pleasant, South Carolina. I knew Dad was slowing down and didn't have quite the energy he used to have. When I moved away in 1989 from Worcester, I never completely left. I was back all the time. In fact, during the summer of 1999 I made three visits to Worcester to spend time with my family. I just hadn't seen it coming. Maybe I was in denial.

It is a Jewish tradition to bury the deceased within two days. The next morning, I flew home by myself. Barbara was going to join me later that evening. All I remember is getting on the airplane and the stewardess escorting me to the front row of first class so I wouldn't have to sit in the back of the plane. When I got off the flight in Boston, Jim McGovern was there to drive me to our family home in Worcester. On Wednesday morning we had the funeral. On the day of the funeral, the regional daily paper, *The Worcester Telegram*, had come out with three feature stories on Dad, and I'm not even counting the one that was on the obituary page. I had prepared a eulogy on the flight. When I got up to speak, I didn't want to stop talking about Dad. I was still in total shock. My whole body had shut down. It was the worst day of my life. I don't even remember what I said.

Another tradition of my faith is called sitting shiva. For one week you stay in the home after the funeral, and friends of the family stop by the home in the evening to pay their respects. What I did during four straight days after the funeral was sit by myself in the neighborhood chapel of Temple Emanuel. I wasn't prepared to even live one day without Dad. It was dreadful for me to sit in the evening in our family home that week and listen to our friends share their favorite stories of Charlie. All I wanted to do was curl up in a corner and cry. My mom knew immediately after Dad passed that I was going to take it the hardest.

I decided to take a leave of absence from work for a month and keep the store open for the holiday season by myself. This was the only thing that made sense to Barbara and me. Barbara knew I couldn't come back to South Carolina right away. While I was keeping the store open, I was working to sell the store and the building Dad owned.

The month at the store went well. My best childhood friend, Joel Greenberg, stopped by every noontime so we could have lunch together at the Jewish deli near Charlie's Surplus on Water Street. This meant so much to me. Joel and I had been extremely close growing up. Dad's friends are still mine also. I do not remember how business went that month. I was preoccupied with my own thoughts. It was awesome that so many people stopped by to pay their respects. While I was in his store, I was doing well. At the end of each day, though, when I locked the door, it was brutally tough.

Fortunately, while I was home, I found a buyer for both the building and the business. Our family friend Charlie Bibaud, who owned Kangaroo Crossing in downtown Worcester, and I made the deal over coffee and a handshake, just as Dad would have wanted it. No lawyers or real estate salespeople were present. This was the best thing that could have happened. The moment I turned over the store's keys to the Bibaud family, I lost it again. My dad's dream, which he had worked his whole life to cultivate, had been turned over to someone else. My mom and my three siblings would have been in a bind, though, if I hadn't made the deal during the month, I was home.

Returning to South Carolina was a relief. I was excited about seeing Barbara and getting some rest. My sister-in-law was planning a New Year's Eve party in two days, and I didn't want to disappoint Barbara, so I rented a tux and went along. The ball dropped at midnight, and I dropped with the ball. It just wasn't the right time to try and celebrate a new millennium for me.

There is one story that will explain what a character Dad was. One-night in 1976 Dad decided to take everyone working at Charlie's out after work for a few beers at the PNI Club near Water Street. The PNI is where Dad took his basketball teams for beers after every game, they played at Crompton Park. It was also the club where he held his road race meetings.

Someone mentioned that pro wrestling was in town that night at the Worcester Auditorium. Around nine at night, Dad left the PNI and told us he'd be back in a little while and not to leave until he returned. At around ten-thirty, the PNI doors swung open and in walked world-famous wrestlers "Bugsy" McGraw, whose nickname was "The

Skull," and Ivan Koloff, nicknamed "The Russian Bear," with Charlie Epstein walking behind them with the biggest smile. We never even thought of asking how he got them to follow him back to the PNI. It's not likely they were given a chance to say no.

After we had been partying with the two giants for about two hours, all craziness broke loose. The tables and chairs were pushed aside, and there were all Charlie's workers rolling around the floor, having a tag team WWW wrestling match with Bugsy and Ivan. I have photos still of this night, taken to prove it. Dad wasn't just standing around watching, he was right in the middle of all the action.

Just before Dad passed, we had a conversation about having a monument honoring him and his road race erected at the finish line of Charlie's Road Race in Elm Park. Elm Park has huge historical meaning in America. It is the first public parcel of land in America put aside as a public park. Dad thought it would be a nice way to honor the race. Charlie didn't like a lot of attention, so he asked me to wait until he wasn't around anymore before I did anything.

The mayor of Worcester, Tim Cooney, is a family friend of the Epstein's. He passed a resolution in city council to have a memorial monument placed at the finish line in Elm Park honoring Dad and the race.

Several years went by before I contacted Mayor Cooney again to tell him I was ready to organize and sponsor a big celebration and un-veiling of the memorial monument. The Worcester Parks Department people were incredible. They wanted this monument erected also. There was no hesitation at all. The monument and plaque had been designed in my mind for almost twenty years.

The day of the event was going to be spectacular. The mayor's office announced that Sunday, June 2, 2019, was going to be called "Charlie Epstein Day" in the city of Worcester. It was surreal to me that twenty years after Dad's passing, his legacy was never going to be forgotten. He was going to have his own special place in Elm Park for eternity. From peddler to icon, he had made his entire group of friends and family proud.

On that Sunday, the greatest collection of world-class runners from all over came back to honor Dad. Four-time Boston Marathon champion, the legendary Bill Rodgers, along with Boston Marathon champions Jack Fultz and Geoff Smith, joined other famous athletes for the festivities. Yes, many of the celebrity champions of the past were present, but many runners from around New England who had aged quite a bit came with their children and grandchildren to share stories about days gone by in Worcester when they had shared the roads with legends like Bill Rodgers, Joan Benoit, Johnny Kelley, Patti Catalano, Geoff Smith, Greg Meyers, Lynn Jennings, and so many more. It turned out to be a beautiful afternoon with a crowd of friends and family, many of whom I hadn't seen since grade school.

The master of ceremonies was none other than Mayor Tim Cooney.

City Counselor Krystian King read a proclamation declaring the day "Charlie Epstein Day" in Worcester and gave the proclamation to my sister Diane, whose photo was the front-page feature in the *Worcester Telegram* the next day.

Bill Rodgers and other runners, along with family friend Rich Hebner, helped the family unveil the monument. Then the party started. My longtime friend Rocin' Ric Porter and the Sons of the Soil Band, consisting of eight musicians, took over the stage and put on a two-hour free concert for the people of my hometown. After the concert we had a catered dinner party at a nice hall nearby. Everyone was invited, and those who came were able to spend time with the greatest group of long-distance runners from the 1970s and 1980s.

Pride, honor, and humility were just a few of the emotions I was feeling that day, in addition to being overwhelmed and pleased. Not only did I have a day to honor my favorite hero, I was also able to use the occasion of the memorial monument to recognize so many other dads who had grown up in the depression years, joined the service, and had come back home to Worcester to raise their families. The Charlie Epstein–Charlie's Road Race Memorial Monument at Elm Park represents the greatest generation.

Driving away from Elm Park after all the festivities were over, I felt a sense of comfort that I had not even thought about before that day. I was home again. I had come full circle from the day I had left Worcester thirty years earlier, and things had never changed. Worcester felt like home for me once again.

My mom, Sarah Epstein, passed away on her birthday, October 21, 2004. I owe so much to my mom. I know this book has a great amount of history about Dad. The absolute truth of the matter is that I was just as loyal to my mom. I spoke with her almost every day of my life. When I returned home after I moved away, I was home very often for visits with her. It was just a slightly different relationship with Dad. Dad and I bonded over sports. Without Mom I would not have accomplished anything, and I would not have had the life I have today.

I am extremely grateful and think about both my parents every day. Mom had a strong spirit, and if I hadn't had that part of her in me, I would have been doomed early on. Still, at times I feel awful that I moved away while my daughters were young, and my parents had to wait for me to return to Worcester to visit with their grandchildren.

If I constantly dwelled on every regret I have, I would not have been able to function over the past thirty-two years. I refuse to live my life like that. In fact, on my last visit with my mom, two weeks before she passed away, she asked me to never look back. I can honestly say when I do look back, I think about my mom just as much as my dad.

Twenty

ARen'T You BILL RUSSELL?

There is nothing that disturbs me more than looking back at the time during which my generation was growing up and comparing it to the world we live in today. Especially when it comes to sports. It is flat-out depressing. How could we have let this happen?

AAU now controls all our youth sports. Parents get sucked into thinking little Johnny and sweet Suzie are going to receive college scholarships. By the time, these young athletes are seniors in high school, parents have spent a fortune so they can play sports. When they don't receive the scholarships, parents start looking for someone to blame.

It happens all the time. The amount of money spent on travel teams is incredible. Colleges don't even recruit their athletes out of high schools anymore. The recruiting is done over the summer, during evaluation periods that are set aside for these AAU showcases.

Unfortunately, parents who don't have a lot of resources feel lots of pressure to spend money that would be better off going toward their child's education.

For years I have been waiting for everything to turn back to when my generation came along. There is no way the young athletes of today are as tough as my generation was. They might be better athletes because of the training techniques and tools they have available to them, but when it comes to toughness, it's not even close.

143

There are lots of reasons children can't walk to a park or playground and spend all day playing and competing without an AAU coach or their moms and dads monitoring their every movement. That is totally understandable. I hear some coaches say kids today are the same as they were thirty and sixty years ago. That is irresponsible thinking. Society, technology, and parenting have made it, so our current high school graduates enter college without having ever organized a game on their own. Today, athletes don't play in a game unless an AAU coach, high school coach, or other adult organizes and supervises the game for them. For many reasons this entitled generation of millennial and Generation Z athletes has made it difficult to coach them when they leave AAU competition behind. Ask any college coach. It takes a college coach a full year to get his athletes to leave their behaviors of entitlement behind. If they can't leave their behaviors behind, they end up transferring. It all started when these AAU travel teams began popping up twenty-five to thirty years ago.

Adidas, Nike, Under Armour, and other sneaker and gear representatives saw this AAU era as the perfect place and time to market their brands. Oh man, did this turn out to be a big mess.

I hear it all the time from my friends in the coaching profession today. They hate having to meet with a lot of these AAU coaches and street agents to recruit a player. In fact, so many of my friends have left the profession because of this cesspool of activity. The only time a college coach stops by the home high school of a recruit is to pick up a transcript. Most of the time, the high school coach is bypassed when one of his student-athletes is being recruited. It's gotten so bad that some athletes skip their high school seasons altogether to better prepare for the AAU season.

It took me many years to accept that our world of sports will never go back to the way it was. Because of this I very rarely attend a game. Some people think the athletes of today are better players than those of my generation. Yes, most are stronger more athletic, and faster because of the training that is available today compared to twenty or fifty years ago. Under no circumstances are they better players, though. Playing under the team concept and being fundamentally sound, my generation was lightyears ahead of today's players. It is not even close.

I made a giant mistake a few years ago. I posted a tweet that disrespected a high-level AAU basketball organization in Charleston. Well, in fact I was completely off base. If I had a son today, that organization might be the only one I would let him play for. They do it the right way. They have educators and high school coaches running their organization. They don't let any shoe representatives get close to their athletes, and best of all they don't milk the families for every penny they can get out of them. I was wrong. I owe the president of their organization an apology in person.

Sometimes I laugh over the salaries of coaches in all sports at major universities. The coaches are treated like living gods until they lose a couple of games. A great example of this is Roy Williams, the basketball coach at the University of North Carolina, and Dabo Swinney, the football coach at Clemson University. Three years ago, Coach Williams won the NCAA Men's Basketball Championship. It was the third national championship for Coach Williams over a fourteen-year period at his alma mater. This past season North Carolina was not particularly good, and a lot of people thought he should be fired.

Dabo Swinney was named the football coach of Clemson over ten years ago. Many in the school's fan base were upset because he was not their first coaching choice. Well, after a slow start in his coaching career, Dabo has won two national championships in the past four years. He now walks on water and receives a salary of over nine million dollars per year. The pay scale for some of these coaches has become ridiculous. The pressure they are under is insane though.

Since I stopped playing several years ago, I have enjoyed traveling around the country in the summers working at my friends' basketball camps, run through the colleges at which they work. Not only does this give me a chance to catch up with my buddies in the coaching profession, but it's also always easy for me to have a blast with the kids after they are dropped off by their parents.

When I left high school coaching a few years ago, the only part I missed was the camaraderie I had been able to develop with almost every player I ever coached. I was like a big, overgrown kid after school at practice with them. I had a blast. I don't think I could have had any more fun than I did. I often look back with a smile and hope my former players are doing well and staying out of trouble. The games became secondary. In fact, I never let my players or other coaches know this, but I didn't enjoy the games at all. Spending Friday nights in Walterboro, Goose Creek, Beaufort, and Monk's Corner just didn't do it for me anymore. It wasn't fair to my players for me to think like that, so I got out. I haven't been back to a high school game since I retired five years ago, so obviously I don't miss it. I'll say this about my coaching career—my teams never had one losing season. I don't miss some of the other coaches. The relationships were only out of convenience, and I was never fooled into thinking otherwise.

Brian Hammel—make no mistake about it, he's my guy. We have had a close friendship for almost forty years. I'm not going to say a lot about his playing career. Brian has always remained humble and doesn't like too many people talking about his career; this guy could teach a lesson on how to move on. The only thing I'll say—in my opinion, in the history of college basketball in New England, Brian Hammel is right up there alongside the greatest college point guards in New England college basketball history.

Brian came out of Bentley University just outside of Boston in the mid-70s. We met playing against each other at Crompton Park. When Brian took over the head coaching job at Bentley three years after he graduated from his alma mater, I started coaching his players during the summer in the Worcester Summer League.

For the rest of Brian's years in New England (before he was recruited away by Coach George Raveling at the University of Iowa to be his assistant), we were extremely close. Brian is who I hung with. We became boys. I scouted for his teams during his seasons coaching at Bentley College. Also, I tried to get to as many of his games as I possibly could.

Brian sent to me a round-trip plane ticket to spend a week with him and his family in Los Angeles. The ticket came the day after I told him in 1987 that I had just received divorce papers delivered to my parents' home. He didn't even tell me he was mailing me the plane ticket. It arrived the next day in an overnight FedEx envelope.

There have been many, many road trips taken over the years to watch Brian's teams play or to just play golf while he was the head basketball coach at Northern Illinois University. New Orleans, Miami Beach, Chicago, LA, Las Vegas, Virginia Beach, Kiawah Island, Lake Tahoe, Richmond are just a few of the destinations to which I've traveled to hang out with my boy. Our friendship is a lot deeper than basketball. We must have played at least one hundred rounds of golf together over the years, and it just kills me to say I have never beaten him once. I've come close, but as they say, "no cigar."

My two biggest thrills in basketball have come from my relationship with Brian. Over the years I have become friendly with almost all of Brian's assistants and several who he worked with over seven years as an assistant at both Iowa and the University of Southern California.

At Northern Illinois one of Brian's assistants was Ryan Marks. Ryan is a tremendous coach. Part of his coaching résumé is a four-year stint as the head coach at the University of Texas–Pan American, a division-one college in Texas. In 2005 Ryan was an assistant coach for Herb Brown (legendary Coach Larry Brown's brother) for Team USA during the World Maccabiah Games in Israel.

The Maccabiah Games are the second-oldest Olympic-style competition in the world. They are commonly referred to as the Jewish Olympics. The athletes represent their native countries in individual and team competition. Swimmer Mark Spitz, Larry Brown, Dolph Schayes and his son Danny, Lenny Krayzelburg, Mitch Gaylord, and Ernie Grunfeld are just famous American Olympians who have also participated in the Maccabiah Games. When I was younger, I was like any other Jewish kid who played basketball seriously—I was always hoping someday I could represent America in the Maccabiah Games in Israel.

Coach Ryan Marks called me one night in June of 2006. His first words were, "how quickly can you pack to go to Sydney, Australia, as the assistant basketball coach for *Team USA* in the Maccabiah Games that are being held there in three weeks?" I was shocked. I told him I was ready to go immediately. Coach Marks had been the first choice as the assistant coach, but he couldn't go. They had asked him to find a replacement assistant. My dream had come true. I was going to represent my faith, country, my favorite sport, and Dad in the World Maccabiah Games in Australia.

Training camp was in two weeks in Valencia, California, at the College of the Canyons. From Los Angeles we would depart for Sydney as an American contingent of athletes and coaches from all sports. The bonus for me was Valencia was the new hometown of my boy, Brian Hammel. Three years earlier I had been to Valencia to let Brian beat me in two rounds of golf. It was going to be a sensational trip.

Sydney is awesome. It reminds me of a mini New York or Atlanta. As a team we had a blast. Team USA in basketball was exceptionally good. We won all seven of our games rather easily. On our tenth day in Sydney, we won the gold medal game against Canada.

The men who played for Team USA were outstanding college basketball players, most of whom were on scholarships and starters at division one universities in America. Our players represented the University of Tennessee, Bowling Green, Princeton, Villanova, North Carolina at Wilmington, St. Mary's in California, Tennessee Tech, Brown University, and a few division- two and division-three colleges.

Our best player was the University of Rochester's Seth Hauben, who had been named Division Three Player of the Year the previous year. Seth had just finished playing his first year as a pro in Norway. He was from Boston, and take my word for it, every New England division one college basketball program missed out on this guy big-time.

The head coach was Harris Adler, who has just spent several years as Bruce Pearl's assistant at Auburn University. All the players and coaches had a blast together. We all developed great chemistry in training camp. When it was time to have my gold medal draped around my neck, whose photo do you think I pulled out of my pocket? Charlie Epstein came with me everywhere I went from the time I left Charleston until I returned home. I never forgot.

When I returned home, many of my friends wanted to know exactly how good I thought our team was. As a team we had talked about it over beers the night we won the gold medal in Sydney. The consensus was that had we played in mid-major conferences such as the Southern Conference or America East Conference, we would have finished in the middle of the pack among ten universities. We could play a little, trust me.

Brian called me one afternoon in September of 2007. He told me to go online and look up a web page address he had me write down and call him back. I was busy with work and forgot to do it. The next day he called and said, "You didn't call me back." I told him I had forgotten, so he told me to look online again for the web page of "Bill Russell and Friends." I saw that Bill Russell, my basketball hero from youth, was hosting an adult basketball camp in Las Vegas. The cost of the camp for anyone who wanted to attend the four-day camp was twenty thousand dollars. I told Brian I couldn't afford to go, but it did look impressive. The counselor-coaches who were being advertised were the most legendary basketball players in the history of the sport. Kareem Abdul-Jabbar, Magic Johnson, Jerry West, Larry Bird, Oscar Robertson, Sam Jones, Julius "Dr. J" Erving, Charles Barkley, Clyde Drexler, and John Havlicek. That's forty-eight NBA championship rings housed at one time at the Wynn Resort.

It looked incredible, but I asked Brian if he was willing to spend twenty thousand dollars. He said, "I don't have to; I'm the camp director, and you're coming as my assistant." I told you Brian and I were boys!

I walked into my kitchen in total shock. I took a week off from work and flew to Vegas the night before camp started. Brian introduced me to eleven-time NBA Champion Bill Russell from the Boston Celtics. Leading up to the week of camp, I was nervous as to how I was going to help direct this camp with this group of megastars. After my first dinner encounter with Coach Russell, I knew immediately I was going to feel right at home. Coach Russell is one of the nicest human beings I have ever had the pleasure of developing a personal bond with. The two of us had a blast together. He told me several funny jokes that I can't repeat in this book. Some of the best laughs I have ever enjoyed were with Coach Russell. As I was falling after one of his jokes, he was letting out one of his famous great big, loud cackles. He treated me like a little brother during those four days. Before anyone wonders, I will say that I do not refer to Bill Russell by his first name. I only refer to him as Coach Russell. Also, do not ask Coach Russell about basketball. In fact, do not ask him anything. If he gets comfortable with you, just sit back, and take in all his stories of race relations, growing up, traveling, and current player salaries and just a lot of teasing. That is Coach Russell. One camper asked Coach Russell what Nelson Mandela thought about his eleven championships. His answer was pure Coach Russell. He said, "Nelson Mandela doesn't give a —— about my championships." I am glad it wasn't me who asked that question. For any reader who may wonder if I really did develop a bond with Coach Russell, the answer is absolutely, or I wouldn't write it in this book.

On the last day of camp, Coach came over to me and put his arm around my shoulder and told me that he wanted me to return to his camp every year because I was his kind of real people. I became emotional when he said that to me.

I'm going to list my favorite memories from each famous counselor I worked with that week. Larry Bird and Oscar Robertson couldn't make it because they had scheduling conflicts. There were so many other legends that attended, it didn't matter.

Julius "Dr. J" Erving: Julius is such a down-to-earth gentleman. He is such a nice guy; he doesn't have any big-time attitude about him. In fact, that week no one did. I hit it off immediately with Julius when I mentioned his former teammates at UMass were friends of mine. It was great to have that in common with Dr. J. The conversations came easily after that.

The best story from camp involved Julius telling us about the first time he met Bill Russell; at the time Julius was a freshman at UMass Amherst. Coach Russell told the UMass coach he wanted to meet Julius Erving. The meeting was held before a Celtics game in Boston at the old Boston Garden in 1968. The first thing coach Russell asked a young Julius as he walked into the locker room was, "what is the most important building on a college campus?" When Julius replied it was the gym, Coach Russell said, "go find the library and start studying."

John Havlicek: "Hondo," as he had been called during his great Celtics career, was the most soft-spoken superstar athlete I have ever gotten to know. He was extremely easy to establish a relationship with. John recently died, what a horrible loss. It was such a treat to have lunch with Hondo, Sam Jones and my buddy Brian after the camp ended. They shared with me many stories of my favorite memories growing up as a big Celtics fan.

Charles Barkley: Charles was my favorite to have fun with. What you see is what you get. One night we went into the casino together, and I watched him for a while at the craps table. I decided it would be best if I met up with him later that night at the club on the bottom floor of the Wynn. He wasn't the one to teach me how to gamble. Before camp was over, he was telling me I needed to get hypnotized if I wanted to improve my golf swing.

Clyde Drexler: He was just like he seems. He got along well with all the campers and was a quiet guy. You could tell he enjoyed himself because he did more coaching with his team than the other coaching legends, except for Kareem.

Kareem Abdul-Jabbar: Kareem was a little standoffish for the first day or so. After I told him his high school coach Jack Donohue from New York was a family friend, we hit it off beautifully. Coach Donohue moved to Worcester to coach Holy Cross after Kareem left high school and went to UCLA. I also told Kareem I had worked at Jack Donohue's camp in New York while I was in college. After that he could not stop talking to me for the rest of camp about the six summers he had spent at the camp while growing up. One day after camp, Kareem pulled me aside and demonstrated a couple of his famous post up moves. He also showed me how to teach high school players how to defend someone playing in the post. No, he did not shoot his sky hook on me. The defense I played on him was more than he could handle. What impressed me about Kareem, besides his basketball ability, was his level of intelligence. Kareem had just written a book about the history of the basketball team the Harlem Renaissance. The team was founded in the 1930s and has a lasting place in American history. It was a fascinating story that I had never heard. Kareem also explained to me that he has used his platform as a basketball icon to speak out against institutionalized racism in America.

Jerry West is a funny guy. A very funny guy. I'm going to pass on sharing his funny stories. Jerry did me a big favor. I got my brother Bobby on the phone with Jerry, and Bobby got to spend a few minutes speaking with his favorite childhood hero.

Sam Jones: Sam was given the nickname "too late" when he teamed with Coach Russell and John Havlicek on the Celtics dynasty teams of the fifties and sixties. He explained to me that he got the nickname from playing against Wilt Chamberlain. Sam explained that every time he would shoot over Wilt and the shot went in, he would yell "too late" in Wilt's face. A classic NBA story.

Magic Johnson: The only way to describe Magic is that he truly is everyone's best friend. The consummate pro. He's also a big hugger! You can understand quickly after spending some time with Magic why he has become such a huge business success since he retired from playing.

Coach Russell never had the camp again because he lost some money on it, so my experience was one and done. But not really one and done. Bill Russell and Friends Adult Fantasy Basketball Camp will always be the greatest experience of my life.

My favorite part of the camp remains the fact that I never heard one word of bragging from even one of these legends. We knew who they were, and they knew who they were. There was not one moment in which anyone relived his glory days with anyone. Basketball had brought us all together for five days, and everyone just enjoyed getting to know one another and building personal bonds. What a relief compared to having to listen to people talk about their high school glory days.

When I returned to Charleston, I sold a basketball for $4,000 that had been signed for me by all the legends. The money was used as seed money to start a scholarship at WAHS for seniors to help pay college costs. The name of the scholarship was the Larry Trevino Scholarship Fund. Larry was a beloved staff member at WAHS who had passed away the year before. During the six years WAHS had the scholarship fund, $22,000 was raised and distributed to twenty-two students.

In the summer of 2013, Brian invited me to attend an incredible gala dinner and golf tournament in Los Angeles. The proceeds of the annual event helped to support the Pump Family Cancer Center at Northridge Hospital, where Brian currently works as president.

It would be impossible to name all the celebrities who attended. Let's just say for starters that Kevin Hart, Jamie Foxx, and Denzell Washington represented Hollywood. Jim Brown, Gale Sayers, Eric Dickerson, Willie McGinest, Michael Irvin, Ronnie Lott, Bo Jackson, Marcus Allen, and Earl Campbell represented the NFL. Julius Erving (we both enjoyed seeing each other again), Ralph Sampson, David Robinson, Chris Mullin, Moses Malone, and Jamaal Wilkes represented the NBA. Representing Major League Baseball were Barry Bonds, Roger Clemens, Gary Sheffield, Rollie Fingers, Ozzie Smith, and Joe Torre. Brian had reserved a room for me at the Beverly Hilton for two nights.

I sometimes have to remind myself of how far this Worcester boy has come from that dreadful ride from Worcester to Charleston back in 1988 when all I was trying to do was to make it to the next day. I am truly blessed to have the support system I had watching out for me. I still speak with Bian but our visits have slowed. I know though that he'll always have my back if I ever need him for something.

In 2013 my brother Eppy, my dad, and I were inducted into the New England Basketball Hall of Fame as a family. Our family friend, the former UConn coach Dee Rowe, nominated the entire family. It was the only way I would have wanted to be inducted. We were inducted into the semipro category for the championship days that Charlie's Surplus had during the legendary run at Crompton Park. It was my job to sell tickets and organize and recruit the big names in New England basketball history to attend.

It was the reunion to end all reunions. Over two thousand people attended this gala induction dinner and ceremony, which was held at the DCU Convention Center in downtown Worcester. It was a who's who of New England basketball.

Kentucky coach John Calipari accepted his invitation and was honored as the legendary head coach from UMass, his first head coaching job. Boston Celtics legend Tom Sanders attended and was honored for his role in helping lead the Celtics to eight NBA championships during his playing days. Boston College coach and former pro basketball star Al Skinner sat among his former UMass teammates. NBA star Ryan Gomes attended and represented Providence College of the Big East Conference. Perry Moss who played for Jim Calhoun at Northeastern and then for the 76'ers attended. One of my favorite Holy Cross players Garry Witts who played for the Washington Bullets after he graduated from "The Cross" came back into town for the festivities. Massachusetts high school legend Chris Herron who played point guard for the Celtics was honored along with Donnie Nelson the General Manager of the Dallas Mavericks. NBA all-star Michael Adams also represented Boston College of the Big East. Harvard Coach Tommy Amaker attended and received the New England Coach of the Year Award. Chris Dailey, the assistant coach for the UConn Lady Huskies' legendary national championship teams, was also honored.

In the last presentation of the night, I had the honor of presenting my dear friend and mentor Togo Palazzi, the legend from Holy Cross and the Boston Celtics, with the Lifetime Contribution to New England Basketball Award.

There is one other Charleston event that I'm very proud to have been involved in. The ESPN Charleston Classic is a major college basketball tournament held at the College of Charleston's TD Arena every year during the week before Thanksgiving. Eight of the top college basketball powerhouses in America come to downtown Charleston for three days and play in what has become one of the country's best in-season tournaments.

After its first three years, the tournament was going to cease. The College of Charleston and the University of South Carolina are part of a huge football state, and the attendance for the basketball tournament had been dreadful. The host of the tournament was coaching legend Bobby Cremins. We had become friendly during his five seasons coaching at the College of Charleston. Bobby reached out to me and asked me if I had any ideas to increase the attendance. In fact, I did. I thought that having high school bands adopt a team and play as the college's pep band throughout the tournament would improve the atmosphere in the arena. The other idea was to sell groups of tickets to businesses and allow those companies to designate public schools in Charleston that they wanted to have attend. This became a big win-win situation! Our attendance nearly doubled during the first year, and the crowds have gotten bigger and bigger every year. Georgetown, Villanova, North Carolina State, University of Massachusetts, Boston College, Wake Forest, University of Connecticut, Florida, Louisiana State University, Florida State, University of Miami, and Clemson are just a few of the many basketball powerhouses that have played in the Classic at least once. The University of South Carolina I hope never comes back because without a doubt they bring the fewest number of fans. Remember, I live in a football state now.

Over the last few years, I have stopped working on the tournament committee. The ESPN staff continues to be gracious towards me though. They reserve a spot for me on the press row every year. This way I get my annual basketball fix, and I can catch up with my many friends who are still involved with my favorite sport.

Twenty-One

"We've Come A Long Way, But We Still Have A Long Way To Go"

After I retired and once my health returned, I knew there was still a lot of work to be done. Representative Wendell Gilliard's name was constantly in the news as a leader. Representative Gilliard was not only a leader for Blacks but also one who was willing to take on a cause if it was for the betterment for all people. When I was at St. John's High, I asked someone on the staff about him; this person told me that I should stay away from him. Unfortunately, I listened to that person and did not contact him at that time.

It had been on my mind for many years that I should get the dropout age changed from seventeen to eighteen in the public schools of South Carolina. This was something I had expected to happen before I retired. It didn't make sense that it hadn't happened during my career. Senator Marlon Kimpson from Charleston is a good friend of mine. I mentioned the dropout age problem that I had been experiencing during my work as a school counselor. He recommended that I call Representative Gilliard and meet with him.

When Representative Gilliard and I finally met over breakfast, we realized that our missions were similar. A close friendship ensued, and before long we were meeting regularly and uniting in many causes, not just the dropout age one.

Representative Gilliard coached me every step of the way and explained to me whom I needed to speak to so we could have a bill drawn up at the State House in Columbia and how to work with legislatures on the state level.

Representative Gilliard is one of the most remarkable men I have ever met. There is no one for whom I have more respect. So many times, I have asked myself, *why did I ever listen to the staff member at St. John's High?* My only regret regarding Representative Gilliard is that we didn't have that initial breakfast many years earlier.

Over the next five years we became like brothers. We could talk about and learn from each other on every topic imaginable. What amazes me about Representative Gilliard is he does not slow down. The second he finishes his work on one issue, he gets right back on his horse to work on another.

Some of Representative Gilliard's achievements are legendary in Charleston and in South Carolina more generally. As a city councilman, he worked to improve the living wage for city employees. He constantly works for economic equality for everyone. He put computers in socioeconomically depressed areas of the city of Charleston, so children from those areas would have better access to them. He started a mission to improve the quality of life for the elderly by making sure anyone who needs an air conditioner and cannot afford one would be given one free of charge through his Cool Breeze program. Wendell spends a great deal of time working with the Department of Housing and Urban Development. The gentrification situation that is now underway throughout America is of grave concern to my friend. It was at the state level that he brought about one of his many bills, the Body Camera Bill, which has equipped all police across South Carolina with body cameras to support their law enforcement work. He has received many awards and commendations for his achievements over the years.

After I retired in 2016, Representative Gilliard presented me with my most treasured award, The Martin Luther King Picture Award for the Lowcountry of South Carolina.

With Representative Gilliard's guidance, I started a crusade across the entire state of South Carolina to get the school dropout age changed to eighteen. That was a mission unlike any other I had undertaken prior to that point. I met with the governor, congressmen, business executives from *Fortune* 500 companies, media outlets of every type, school superintendents, mayors, principals, state representatives, and even lobbyists. I did not leave one single stone unturned. The nice part is that Representative Gilliard was by my side every step of the way. For four years this mission became my full-time job. I wasn't afraid of anyone's position or rank or opinion. The Charleston *Post and Courier* even published three editorials in favor of raising the age to eighteen. A group of state legislators led by Representatives Gerry Govan, David Mack, and Gilliard put a bill together in Columbia that missed going forward by one vote. It is important to note that my wife Barbara was part of this mission, working side by side with us every step of the way. Barbara is a retired middle school counselor who believed in everything we were trying to accomplish. She has always felt strongly that teenagers should not be allowed to stop attending school and drop out without a parent's permission.

After narrowly failing to move the bill along, I worked even harder to get it passed during the next legislative session. During fifteen trips back and forth from Charleston to Columbia to lobby for my bill, Representative Gilliard and I traveled together. The trip is two hundred- and twenty-miles round trip.

The next vote came with more momentum. After I testified for the second time before the state education subcommittee, a second vote was taken, and this time the vote was unanimous in our favor. This is where I thought we had it passed. The day the bill was to be heard by the full committee, though, a member of the legislature asked for it to be delayed because he wasn't going to be in attendance and wanted to be present when it was heard. We were devastated when the two-year session ended, and they ran out of time to reschedule the bill. It was again tabled for this past year, but because of the coronavirus it hasn't yet been heard.

After four years of effort by many people who believed so strongly in what we were set to accomplish, we were back to square one. I cannot even begin to explain how badly I wanted this bill to pass and become law. I was crushed!

We had been so close to our goal that I had felt it in the palm of my hand, and then it was just taken right away from us. Eventually the bill will go into law, but someone else will have to get behind it because I am truly worn out. I know Barbara is as well.

I'll tell you what I noticed about several state representatives who had mixed feelings about the bill. They were racially profiling against some of the students who might benefit from an age increase. I could see it clearly in their faces.

Wendell and I have worked on other projects together. A year ago, Representative Gilliard and I released a speech by Reverend Dr. Martin Luther King that he had given in 1961 in my hometown of Worcester, at Congregation Temple Emanuel, which I had attended growing up. Laura Klein found it tucked away in her grandfather's personal belongings. Laura's grandfather, Rabbi Joseph Klein, had been the longtime rabbi at the temple. Laura was willing to share this historic find with the students of Charleston. Wendell and I had a big press conference in downtown Charleston with Coretta Scott King's first cousin, Christine Jackson, in attendance. The conference was attended by all the local news media and many politicians and educators. It is wonderful that this speech is now in the schools in both of my hometowns of Worcester and Charleston.

Two years ago, Wendell and I were joined by our friends, Reverend Kevin Brown, and Carminski Latten, in listening to a Martin Luther King taped speech that a family in Summerville had discovered and wanted us to hear. Wendell and I still say it was the hardest we have ever laughed. Understand that Wendell, Reverend Brown, and I take six-mile walks together two or three times per week. This is the time that we brainstorm new ideas and many times must stop because some of our stories are extremely funny. While we were in the home of the family in Summerville, they played us two tapes. One was the speech Reverend King gave the last time he had been in Charleston in 1967 to help organize the famous hospital workers' strike. The other speech had been recorded by a hidden microphone in a secret Ku Klux Klan meeting held outside of Charleston in the late sixties. There was nothing funny about either tape at all; they were historic finds. What was funny was that while the tapes were being played for us, I was recording everything on my iPhone. At the end of the playback, the owner of the tapes said he was looking for a buyer who would pay a million dollars for both.

The family had given me permission to record the tapes so I could help them find a buyer. The recordings were so muffled that I deleted them three days later. So, there it was: As we were driving back to Charleston, I was playing back both recordings for free on my iPhone while they were still looking for their million-dollar buyer. We were all laughing so hard I had to pull over on the side of the road to regain my composure.

The tapes were finally sold at an auction in New York for $37,000.

Representative Gilliard has taken me across the state on many of his missions. At times I felt like I was his top aide, and maybe I was for a while.

The most difficult situation I found myself in happened when Representative Gilliard and the police chief of Charleston, Luther Reynolds, were at a crossroads over what they perceived to be a case of mutual disrespect. Some of Representative Gilliard's constituents on the Charleston eastside felt that they were not being heard. Chief Reynolds thought Wendell was disrespecting him in public. My opinion with both feeling the way they did was it was a perception caused by lack of communication. During the times I was around Chief Reynolds, I thought of him as a great guy. I thought the same of Wendell.

This situation needed to be corrected quickly. For the betterment of the entire Lowcountry, these two leaders, Wendell, and Luther, had to work on the same page. I approached Chief Reynolds at a local march protesting domestic violence. I offered to sit down with him and Wendell over lunch to help mediate a new working agreement. No one outside the three of us knew anything about the meeting.

We all sat down, and right away I thought I was in over my head. There was a little mistrust between the two men. I thought for sure we would never reach a resolution because the personal divide was real. I wasn't taking sides. What I was trying to do was keep everyone in the room until they made a compromising agreement. There was serious dialogue exchanged in that room. After ninety minutes there was finally a reason to feel optimistic, maybe. A consensus emerged that personal feelings had to be put aside for the betterment of the people of Charleston. At this point another forty-five minutes of peaceful compromises took place, and hands were shaken, and lunch was eaten. That night the three of us attended a community event on the eastside of Charleston, along with four hundred residents. When Wendell got up to speak, he referred to the meeting we had just left as an Ali-Frazier heavyweight fight. He was not kidding. This is the first time I have ever spoken about this incredible experience publicly. Sometimes I don't know how this Jewish guy from Worcester, Massachusetts, has gotten involved in some of the things I have. Chief Reynolds and Representative Gilliard now have a wonderful friendship to go along with a strong working partnership.

Let's hope for a long and productive relationship.

Another enormous accomplishment for Representative Gilliard came during the time this book was being written, June of 2020. Through determination and resolve over many years, he led the charge to have the John C. Calhoun statue removed on June 24, 2020. The monument to this racist vice president from Charleston, who served from 1825 to 1833, had been standing in Marion Square in downtown Charleston for 125 years. I am proud of my friend Wendell.

In the words of the great Reverend Doctor Martin Luther King, Jr., "We've come a long way, but we still have a long way to go."

Twenty-Two

CLOSING THOUGHTS

I wanted to write this story for many reasons. I know I have lived a life that had two separate tales and I wanted to combine them for my daughters, grandchildren, and my friends into one story book form. I also knew I had a story to share of tremendous determination that helped me overcome some incredibly difficult challenges. I'm hoping by speaking out about my late life accomplishments might motivate others who find themselves struggling at a young age. Speaking out for the students in the Lowcountry of SC who have struggled or who continue to struggle was also especially important for me. This book is not only my story it is theirs as well. Lastly, I have always wanted to join the life history of my Dad, Charlie Epstein with the history of my adventures and make it one unique memoir. I hope this book, *THEY CALL ME PATHFINDER; Education-Basketball-Equality*, represents all I have mentioned with integrity.

How can I possibly thank the hundreds of people who have welcomed me into this magical part of America called the Lowcountry? How can I possibly thank the people back in my hometown of Worcester, Massachusetts, for never giving up on me? I am proud, I am honored, and most of all I am indebted to each person I have crossed paths with during my life.

I am the most flawed human being that I know. Every word of this book has come from my own experiences and opinions. I did not write this as a brag book, nor was I trying to change anyone's way of thinking about me or any perception that someone might already have. I wrote the truth as I remember it, my truth, and that truth came directly from the heart. I have tried to give my students who struggled and never earned their high school diplomas a voice.

This was a tough book to write. I've had more than my share of ups and downs. A lot of the downs I blame myself for. There were a couple, though, in which I was the victim. That M&M formula equal success took a while to kick in, in my case. I hope you as a reader maybe learned something from this book, but even if you did not, I hope you found it enjoyable and entertaining. I know I am a bit of a character, and people who have known me for any length of time will tell you that. I am too old now to try and change.

* * *

As in the song "My Way" by Frank Sinatra, I've lived a life that's full and have traveled many roads. Yeah, I guess I did do it my way!

Regrets—I've had a few,

- I wish I had known about my M&M formula equal success when I was younger.
- We came up just a little short in our efforts to change the SC public school dropout age.
- I was never able to get Sonny Price and Malcolm Person inducted into the Worcester State University Athletic Hall of Fame (a miscarriage of justice).
- I wish I hadn't waited forty years to sit down and talk with my first love.

Since retirement I have been working as a nationally certified personal trainer at the Mount Pleasant Senior Center. I enjoy the work and my clients very much.

Acknowledgments

This story has been sixty-eight years in the making.

I would like to thank the following people for their guidance, love, and support they have offered in my pursuit of my dreams. My beautiful wife Barbara and my daughters and their husbands, Brooke and Torrey Marshall, and Karli "Alexis" and Sean Bunnell. My mom and dad, the late Sarah and the late Charlie Epstein, along with my siblings Diane Epstein, the late Bobby "EPPY" Epstein, Trudy and Matthew Epstein, and Beth Epstein, my stepchildren Matt and Lindsay and their spouses Ann Brock and Tom Boger, and all our seven grandchildren we share. A huge thank you to my editor, Carol Peecksen, whom I am trying to make famous (beyond her being related to the late Ernest Hemmingway). I want to recognize Jenny Chandler and the entire staff at Elite Authors Publishing. Much thanks also to LeDonne Brands for their expert marketing of this story.

Much love and gratitude to my nieces Dawn and Faith Sternlieb, Burton and Lois Berg, Brian and Moira Hammel, Jim and Jill Burke, Mayor Tim Cooney and his wife, Joyce, "Butch" and Barbara Ravelson, the late George Query, my fabulous aunt, Bertha Mann and my cousins Mike, Steve, and Barbara-Ellen, the late Don Lemenager and Danny Lemenager, the late John Scott, Togo Palazzi, Coach George Blaney, Coach Jack "The Shot" Foley, Coach Dee Rowe, the late Paul and his brother the late Tom Tivnan, the late Tom Burns, the late Coach Bob Devlin, Tricia, Amy and Mandy Timmons, Marty Lindsay, the late Joe Lonergan, Billy Rodgers, Sharon Barbano, "Ma-Ma" Jan Albrecht, Billy and Maureen Herrion, Jim and Gina McCaffrey,

Representative Wendell Gilliard, Ann Cunningham, Richard and Martha Ulmer and family, the late Floyd Hiott and his wife Anna Hiott, the late Ken Shelton, Toni Kirby, Lynn Reed, Carrie Rittle, the late Candy Bates Quinn, Ginger Reijners, the late Mary Ellen Duffy, Mary and Lee Runyon, Bill and Linda Lynds, John and Debbie Dodds, Tom and Cathy Grundy, Cheryl Deas, Suzannah Countryman, Coach Gregg Marshall, Elizabeth Freedman, Brad Davis, Jim Young, Larry Francoise, the late Kenny and his brother "Augie" Gwozdz, Peter Egan, Reverend Dr Eric Mack, the late Art Andreoli, Mark Smiley, Sandy Pennekamp, Ellyn Winkles, Chuckie Robinson, and his mom Ma-Ma Louise and his wife Gina, Jermaine Scott, Jackie Simmons, Marvin "Spider" Davis, Buddy Beall, Larry Smalls, the Meehan Family (including the late Bill, Ann, the late David, and Mark), the late Thomas and the late Mary McGovern along with the entire McGovern family including "Lil Sis," Malcolm Dewitt, Tom Haddad, the late Coach Bert Hammel, the late John Murphy, the late Steve Gadaire, Manny Quintela, Frank Oftring, the late Owen Mahorn, Franny Laffin, the late Ken Burger, Gene Sapakoff, Coach Ryan Marks, "Lefty" Eurenius, Howie Greenblatt, Tom and Cheryl Conrad, Representative David Mack, Coach Jim Girouard, the late Coach Buddy Masterson, the late John "Doc" Coughlin, Doug Safford, the late Mayor Tom Early and his late wife Rita, Bobby and Dianne Peretti, Nick and Avis Pilson, Joel and Judy Greenberg and the late Betty Greenberg, the late Nick Manzello, Paul Jarvey, Tony "Foots" Jeffries, Kenny Sadowski, Bruce Bindman, the late Chet Chaison, the late Coach Buster Sheary, Laura Klein, Kevin Clark, the late Coach Frank McArdle, Stuart Herman, Aki Stavrou, Christine Jackson, Reverend Kevin Brown, Tom McMillen, Richard Lapchick, Xavier McDaniel, Rick Sanford, Coach Seth Greenberg, Coach Jim Calhoun, "Kapt" Kris Grundberg, Bob Berman, Nick Kotsopoulos, Debbie Antonelli, Geoff Smith, Bob Hodge, Vinny and Donna DelMonte, Chief Luther Reynolds, Dr. Debbie White, Cedric Ball, Jim and Maura Sweeney, the late Bob Bigelow, the late Coach Jack Donohue, Coach Tom McLaughlin, Dick Cerasuolo and his late wife

Mary, the late Coach Ken Coblentz, Steve Hummel, Lynn Shadrix, Joe and Petra Bowler, Jerry and Debbie Baker, Ron Rabonovitz, the late Jim Yates, Eddie and Kathy Reilly, Tommy Haddad, Sophia Barshan, Kathy Shannon Fitzpatrick, Maxine Shulman Bosquet, the late Tom Austin, Peter Bruce, Bill and Marilyn Endicott, Paula Freeman, Scott and the late Marilyn Grueninger, Dave Colwell, Ron Parker, the late Jerry Feldman, Howie Sobel, Renee Rudnick, Wendy and her sister Linda Rickles, my late cousin Johnny Epstein and Neal "Poink" Portnoy.

To all my Lancer brothers and sisters, I was away far too long. It's great to be back with y'all; Mal Person, Rich Riley, Mike Murphy, Jim Ridick, Steve Flynn, Sonny Price, Tim Ethier, Paul Sullivan, Jim McGovern, Artie Gazal, Lennie Kasprzak, Tom Boland, Michael Bagni, Gail Cosky, Mary Sullivan Police, Mary Wannamaker, Gail Hebert, Pat Ethier Marois, and Patricia Glennon.

* * *

At this time, I would like to also acknowledge the athletes who at one time or another wore Charlie's Surplus across their team jerseys. I think of you all often. Let me know, guys, if Charlie still owes any of you "gas" money (*wink*).

To everyone who laced up their running shoes and ran in the Charlie's Surplus Ten-Mile Road Race, Charlie and I thank you.

Love and prayers to everyone, stay safe!

REVIEWS AND ENDORSEMENTS

Christine Jackson, first cousin to Coretta Scott King, says, *They Call Me Pathfinder: Education—Basketball—Equality* is a book everyone should read. Thank you, Mark, for writing this story. You explain why my cousin, Rev. Dr. Martin Luther King Jr., used to say, "We've come a long way, but we still have a long way to go, especially when it comes to education in South Carolina."

Xavier "The X Man" McDaniel, all-American NBA all-star, writes, "*They Call Me Pathfinder* is a great book to read because it talks about how to persevere in life and how not to give up. Pathfinder explains ways to continue to work hard and to help others become successful."

Bill Rodgers, America's greatest long-distance runner of all time, writes, "My friend, Pathfinder, does a fantastic job of bringing back to life the Charlie's Surplus Ten-Mile Road Race in Worcester, Massachusetts, one of my favorite road races I have ever won. Awesome book!"

Rick Sanford, all-American in football at the University of South Carolina, first-round draft pick, longtime defensive back for the New England Patriots for the NFL, comments, "What an inspiring read! Mark shows all of us that perseverance is the key when you have setbacks in life. He shows us the good that lies within our souls by his equality for all philosophy. Incredible storytelling by a good and decent man. A must read during these changing of times!"

Aki Stavrou, senior development specialist, African nations peace ambassador, World Bank recommends this book to all young people facing challenges. "Where some are stuck in the present and see only insurmountable obstacles, others see hope and a future. When youth in particular are faced with challenges for which they have no solutions and are confronted with choices in which they do not have the ability to make calculated judgments, what they need is assistance to make the right decisions. As a society, we owe our youth as much support and direction as possible, on their pathway to adulthood. This is what Mark set out to do and more, dedicating twenty-seven years to working with young people, helping them to help themselves. He has done so tirelessly and selflessly, and throughout his journey he has maintained a sense of eternal hope, carried a smile on his face and has always done so with a sense of self-effacing humor. He is not a man whose name you will find in history books nor among those making the news, but if you asked each and every one of the students with whom he worked, they would certainly have volumes of positive stories to tell on how he helped them through their life's experiences. Mark's book comes out at a both frightening and hopeful juncture in our country's history, and I cannot help reflecting on what Steve Jobs once said, 'Everyone here has the sense that right now is one of those moments when we are influencing the future.' I would strongly urge you to read Mark's book, because it will inspire a part of you, in a way that I hope leaves a mark that leads you as the reader to inspire somebody today, so as to influence our collective future."

State Representative Wendell Gilliard, leading human rights activist in South Carolina, writes, "Mark 'Pathfinder' Epstein is a man of altruism, who is educated and also motivated. This book is about a man who has faced his obstacles and has continued to stand tall as he faces the world head on. These challenges molded Pathfinder to become the leader he is today. An amazing but true story!"

Debbie Antonelli, ESPN, CBS Sports college basketball analyst writes, "This book is about listening, learning, and celebrating different. Mark carved a unique and different path because of his love for sharing, engaging, and finding solutions. In this time of change, Mark was a change-agent for different decades ago when it wasn't easy, but right."

Mary Runyon, retired principal of West Ashley High School, Charleston, South Carolina, comments, "As Mark describes his journey in *They Call Me Pathfinder: Education—Basketball—Equality*, it is easy to see how relentless he has been to overcome the challenges of his early adult years to build a better life for others. In retrospect, it is evident that those individuals who stood in his way or who were self-centered were not eligible to be on the Epstein Team! Mark has always stayed in 'forward' motion and 'guarded' his beliefs in the true characterization of a basketball team. His story is filled with a unique energy and charisma that propels the reader into his work and insights."

Ron Rabonovitz, author of Always *Jackie*, which Amazon designated the Top Nonfiction Book for Kids in 2020, writes, "Right from the first page I was hooked. Just a fascinating story of one man's mission to change the world through education."

Formal Editorial Review, "I enjoyed reading your book, which is an entertaining combination of sports, career, family, and new beginnings. Basketball fans and educators in particular will be captivated by your personal experiences with professional athletes, providing youth with hope, and overcoming challenges in the school system."

From Nick Kotsopoulos, Political Columnist for the Worcester Telegram, Finally got a chance to read your book and I want to congratulate you on the job you did. I found your story to be informative, entertaining, and revealing.

I have to say that the early chapters of your book about your time in Worcester really struck a chord with me because of my familiarity with many of the things and people you talked about, from the description of your father and his business, the city of Worcester as a whole, the early days of Charlie's Road Race, Crompton Park, etc. You really nailed it, my friend. You also showed that you are a true Worcester person by describing three-family homes as three-deckers, as people in Worcester call them, and not triple deckers as the Boston media and others refer to them. I think old-time Worcester people, like myself, will really enjoy the stories you told about those days.

I also learned a most interesting thing in your book – how you got the moniker "Pathfinder." I never knew that and it's a great story. And I found so many of your observations to be quite revealing as well. I enjoyed your stories about Jimmy Burke and the Mahorn boys.

The rest of the book about your life in South Carolina I found quite interesting as well because it was a new chapter in your life, and you took on so many worthy causes. It was like a whole different life for you.

I also applaud you for not pulling any punches about your life story; you let it all out there. I learned a lot about you that I did not know before.

In reading your book, I found you to be a cross between George Bailey (the main character in It's a Wonderful Life) – someone who touched so many peoples' lives for the better – and Forrest Gump – someone who is not afraid of doing what he feels is right while also rubbing shoulders with so many well-known people and athletes.

A remarkable story, indeed, and a remarkable job in telling that story. Congratulations and I want to wish you the best of luck with the book. Take care and stay healthy!

Made in the USA
Monee, IL
23 September 2020